Pursuing Open Heavens

Seeking God for Our Generations

Marc Dupont

Sovereign World

Sovereign World
PO Box 777
Tonbridge
Kent TN11 0ZS
United Kingdom

ISBN 1 85240 304 7

Scripture quotations are taken from:

New American Standard Bible. Copyright © 1978 by Thomas Nelson,
Inc. © The Lockman Foundation, 1960, 1962, 1963, 1968, 1971, 1972,
1973, 1975, 1977, La Habra, California.

The Holy Bible, New King James Version. Copyright © 1982 by Thomas
Nelson, Inc.

The Holy Bible, New International Version. Copyright © 1978 by New
York International Bible Society.

The publishers aim to produce books which will help to extend and
build up the Kingdom of God. We do not necessarily agree with every
view expressed by the author, or with every interpretation of Scripture
expressed. We expect each reader to make his/her judgement in the
light of their own understanding of God's Word and in an attitude of
Christian love and fellowship.

Typeset by CRB Associates, Reepham, Norfolk
Printed in the United States of America

Contents

Chapter 1

Holy Prophetic Frustration (part 1)

"A voice says, 'Call out.'
Then he answered, 'What shall I call out?'"
(Isaiah 40:6 NASB)

Waiting on God

In early 1981 I had an encounter with God that basically ruined my well thought-out plans for my life – although, at the time, I did not really understand the implications whatsoever. During that period I was living in San Diego, California, and was actively involved in church leadership in a small congregation that had arisen out of the Jesus Movement. I was attending seminary, auditing basic theological classes and trying to determine whether or not I had the aptitude to study, learn, and teach the Bible.

One Sunday morning our pastor announced that in two weeks time we were going to have a guest speaker who functioned as a "prophet" in the Body of Christ. Although at the time I did believe that supernatural gifts of the Holy Spirit as mentioned in 1 Corinthians 12, were still in effect, I had no perspective at all on New Covenant prophecy. I wasn't quite opposed to it, but really didn't understand the need for it, since the Bible was now complete and all we needed to know could be found in the Scriptures.

As the Sunday in question came nearer I did pray and ask the Lord to help me to be open to anything that was of Him, but I also asked Him to protect me from any deception. The "prophet" spoke at the morning meeting on the topic of gossip and how it can destroy churches, allowing the enemy to make inroads into the life of the church. "This is all well and good," I thought, "the message is biblical, sound, and much-needed." Then, as he closed, he announced that after the evening meeting that night we would have a time of "waiting on the Holy Spirit".

My first thought was, "Why? Does God show up as late for meetings as many of us do? Why should we need to 'wait' for Him – after all, He's always there wherever two or more are gathered. And besides that, all Christians if they are truly born again, have the Holy Spirit within them. So what's the deal?" However, trying to be honest with the Lord, I prayed the prayer I had prayed earlier: "God, I'm asking for eggs and fish, don't let me have any snakes or scorpions" (Luke 11:11–13).

Again, the message he shared that night was a good biblical message – that much I remember. Then he ended the service and stated that, for anyone who wanted to stay behind, there was going to be an "afterglow" meeting. I had never heard that term before. A few people left and then he quietly and calmly said, "Come, Holy Spirit". For the most part, the rest of the meeting, which lasted an hour or so, was quite normal and ordinary. It seemed more a time of worship without singing than anything else. But something was significantly different – you could clearly sense a definite and tangible presence of God in the meeting that had not been there previously. In fact, although I was on my guard against both deception and/or mere emotionalism, there was a sense of God in that meeting that I had not encountered in my previous six years of knowing the Lord Jesus.

The meeting that night, in comparison with thousands of others I've attended since, was not actually all that powerful or radical. There were one or two people so overwhelmed by the power of the Holy Spirit that they were not able to stand – but, all in all, it was rather quiet. It was characterized more by a sense of awe than anything else. In the course of the meeting a young man came up to me who often traveled and ministered with the prophetic minister. I found out later that he was a construction contractor by trade who happened to be an evangelist and also functioned in prophecy. He approached me and asked if he could pray for me saying he had "a word from the Lord for me". That was the first time I had ever heard the phrase, except in discussing biblical stories.

I was a bit apprehensive, but remembered the positive side of my prayer: "Lord, let me be open to anything You really have for me." So I agreed. He asked me to close my eyes and focus on the Lord and then he prayed for an anointing of the prophetic to come over me. I had no idea what this meant. I was ignorant of Paul's encouragement to the church of Corinth to *"desire eagerly spiritual gifts, but especially that you may prophesy"* (1 Corinthians 14:1 NASB). Although my "heresy antennae" was up like a submarine's periscope in enemy waters, I still did not feel that anything really off-the-wall was taking place. Then he said to me, "This is what the Lord says to you, 'What you see him doing [he was pointing to the prophetic minister], that is what God is going to have you do.'" And that was it. He finished and calmly walked away.

I had not shaken, fallen down, or experienced any outward manifestation whatsoever. What is more, I had no idea what this "word" meant, or even if it was truly a "word from God" for me. But one thing was very clear – something significant had just happened within my heart. I had an "inward" sensation, very similar to the one I had experienced when I gave my life to Jesus, and received Him as Lord and Savior – that feeling of my heart being "warmed" as John Wesley once described it. I did not really know *how* to think about it, but I knew as I left the meeting that night, something was *very* different.

Sacred promises

Even though the so-called "prophet" had spoken two theologically correct messages (the sole acid test in those days), I was still not convinced that legitimate prophetic ministry had taken place – even though I had no criteria at that time for even assessing what that might be. But something within me was different and for the better. Even the next morning when I awoke, I still sensed that some sort of divine trans-action had taken place.

Someone has said that the longest distance in the world is approximately 12 inches – the distance from our head to our heart. The best way I can describe what had happened that night is that God had taken a truth that was very much in my head, and supernaturally transplanted it into my heart. The church I had been in for the first five years of my walk with God, the seminary I was studying in, and the church I was currently involved with, all stressed good, basic, biblical theology. One of the basics that I strongly believed in was the sovereignty of God. I believed that God was all-powerful and that Satan, by comparison, was only a created being who had nothing on God whatsoever. And theologically, I believed that God – the Lord God Jehovah – was in control of the church as we yielded our lives to Him. In that context, I also believed that we as Christians did not so much need to *fear* the devil, but as we sought God and lived for Him we would be *"more than conquerors through Him who loved us"* (Romans 8:37 NKJV). In fact, I believed that by His grace and power, we were to be His ambassadors to the ends of the earth. Yet, despite my strong theology of God and His power, most of my views on life were dominated by an irrational and unbiblical understanding of the power of Satan and the antichrist, and the end-times.

I had a very limited view of what could take place in ministry in the years before Christ's return, because my thoughts were consumed with popular church views of what Satan and the antichrist were up to. At the time I had hopes of someday being a pastor who would plant a number of different churches. I had a vague vision of starting a church, getting some people saved, building up the infrastructure and leadership, turning it over to someone else, and then doing it all over again. One problem with that vision was that I was rather out of touch with God's will for my life. My parameters for viewing ministry were more governed by current traditions than the Lord.

Even worse, was my world-view. Although I did have faith for a few more people to be saved and a few more churches to be planted before the Lord returned, my world-view was governed by a focus on the growing sin and decay in world culture. Here I considered myself solidly based on good theology, but the truth was that I was far more confident in Satan's plans to dominate the world than in any ability of God's to pour out His Spirit in a substantial way that could transform today's culture. My head could easily quote 1 John 4:4: *"the one who is in you is greater than the one who is in the world"*, but my heart was governed by a small revelation of God's power and sovereignty. As John Arnott, from Toronto, would put it years later, "My God was too small in my eyes". In my heart of hearts I greatly needed to *"magnify the LORD"* as David did (Psalm 34:3 NASB). David was not saying that we can make God bigger than He is, but when we draw near and worship Him, the eyes of our hearts become enlightened to see Him as He truly is. The prophetic is to the church what a telescope is to an astronomer – it helps us to see the heavenlies as they really are.

A revelation of Jesus

The day after my encounter with the Lord, I went for a run in some hills near where I lived. The rural areas in that part of north San Diego county are mainly hilly, with vineyards, citrus and avocado trees, and dirt roads. I ran that afternoon on a dirt road among some hills – a route I had taken probably fifty times or more. I was still experiencing a certain sense of awe and wonder about God and His Presence from the night before that was startlingly refreshing.

I probably ran for about five miles or so. As I often did when I finished a run, I rested against my pick-up truck to catch my breath. During the last half mile or so I would usually pick up the pace as much as I could and then finish very winded. As I began to catch my breath, I looked around at the scenery – hills I had looked at many, many times before. All of a sudden I saw a sight I had never seen there, or anywhere else before – I saw Jesus and was He ever huge! So huge that He totally dwarfed the hills, the clouds and everything else.

God has ways of showing you the things He wants you to see, and yet preventing you from seeing things you don't need to see. I cannot say what color Jesus' hair or skin were, but I can say that He was huge and that He was smiling at me. It was the most all-consuming smile I had ever seen. It was not a smile of momentary mirth as from a joke or something He saw that was funny. Neither was it a smile of arrogance or condescension. Rather, it was a smile of immense joy that all the happiness to be found in this world could not touch. It was an incredibly confident smile.

They say in the arts and media that a picture is worth a thousand words. My experience of the revelation of God is that one vision can transcend a hundred-thousand words! I was too stupefied to do anything other than gaze at Him. He never actually said anything to me with words, but that smile, combined with the sheer size of Him (He appeared to be about 30,000 ft tall), completely shattered whatever walls I had built in my understanding of what God could or would do in my lifetime. I am not speaking so much of myself, but through His church before His return for His Bride.

I don't think at that precise moment, or even for years to come, I can properly put into words precisely what took place in my heart at that moment, but all of a sudden I realized in my heart that God, in actuality, was the God of biblical theology. Jesus is not the great "I Was" of two-thousand years ago. Neither is He the great "I Will be" who we will meet when we arrive in heaven. He was, is, and shall always be, the great *"I AM"*. I could not have clearly stated it at that moment, but I also realized that God was not afraid for the church. Neither was He afraid of what Satan or the antichrist might do.

He was, in fact, *totally God* and nothing less than that. In fact, far more than that, He conveyed in the language of the heart, that in my lifetime certain sacred promises were going to be at least partially fulfilled – the *"plowman shall overtake the reaper"* and *"the mountains shall drip with sweet wine and all the hills shall flow with it"* (Amos 9:13 NKJV). (Not for nothing was I running in hills predominated by vineyards!) And as Joel prophesied,

> *"I will pour out My Spirit on all mankind ... And your sons and daughters will prophesy, your old men will dream*

dreams, your young men will see visions. And even on the male and female servants I will pour out My Spirit in those days."   (Joel 2:28–29 NASB)

Peter quoted that prophecy on the day of Pentecost, but as yet it has only been partially fulfilled.

The "forerunner" spirit

It is a principle of God that as long as there are "ears to hear, what the Spirit is saying to the church", He will try to reveal what He is about to do before He does it. The prophet Amos confirmed that,

> *"Surely the Lord GOD does nothing, unless He reveals His secret to His servants the prophets."*   (Amos 3:7 NKJV)

He does so for two reasons. Firstly, God calls us to serve Him out of love and friendship. Jesus stated:

> *"I no longer call you servants, because a servant does not know his master's business. Instead, I have called you friends, for everything that I learned from my Father I have made known to you."*   (John 15:15 NIV)

Secondly, through prophetic prayer and proclamation, He often uses people to *"go before"* what He is about to do and prepare the way.

For every fresh move of Jesus there is a "John the Baptist", or a forerunner people. However, just as John operated outside the religious system of his time, forerunners often seem very much at odds with the status quo of the church. They are the ones who somehow, cannot be content with only a few more people being saved. They are the ones who fail to be excited by new church buildings and programs. They are the ones who seem like a broken record in their constant call to pray more and "seek the face of the Lord". They are the ones who are seemingly always rocking the boat.

However, before we examine the forerunner type more, it is very necessary to state the following: There often tends to be little discernment in the church regarding the genuine fore-runner and what I call charismatic goofiness. Unfortunately, there are many who, because of unmet emotional needs, or rebellion and anti-authority problems, go to great lengths to exemplify weird religious behavior. And often when a pastor or church leader attempts to bring correction or balance, that leader is then labeled as "anti prophetic" or one who "quenches the Spirit". Usually what leaders are trying to prohibit is not so much the *prophetic* but the *pathetic*! What many wannabe prophets need to realize is that true wisdom from above is pure (without self-promotion), peaceable (it brings faith and peace, not fear and personal attack) and reasonable (it can be talked through and is not a "black and white" ultimatum – see James 3:17).

Unfortunately, because of personal hurts and other agendas, some prophetic people and intercessors cause more harm than good. Often, the damage they do is to muddy the waters so much with their anti-authority attitudes, that when the "real thing" comes along many pastors are just too skeptical to hear what the Lord is saying prophetically. However, the baby must not be thrown out with the bath water. God is a God who speaks to His children and His friends. He is a God who wants to lead us by His Spirit, rather than by circumstances. There are, unfortunately, some pastors and leaders who do quench the Holy Spirit, but there are numerous pastors, elders, and leaders today who are genuinely seeking God for a genuine harvest to come to their cities.

We know that the Virgin Mary became pregnant with the baby Jesus when the Holy Spirit overshadowed her. I often compare those who have the forerunner spirit with a woman in her seventh or eighth month of pregnancy. Although her husband, relatives, friends, etc., may try to make everything as nice and comfortable as possible for her, she cannot really get any rest until the baby comes forth. The long-awaited child is the only thing will remove her discomfort. Except for other women who have carried babies, or are currently pregnant, no one else can really appreciate that restlessness.

John the Baptist was *"the voice of one crying in the wilder-ness"* (Isaiah 40:3 NKJV). Isaiah prophesied *"Cry out"* in

Isaiah 40:6, and then rhetorically asked *"What shall I cry?"*
When one is captured by a great hunger for a significant
move of God to come to their culture, nothing less will do.
However, the desperation of that cry will usually seem utterly
fanatical to the rest of the church. It will seem fanatical, at
times, even to the one crying out!

1 Corinthians 2:9 reads,

> *"Things which eye has not seen and ear has not heard, and
> which have not entered the heart of man, all that God has
> prepared for those who love him."*   (NASB)

Often the prophetic cry of the prayer-warrior and prophet
seems a bit absurd even to themselves. After all, with the
growing problem of sin and destruction in our world culture,
it does seem extremely illogical to believe we should seek
God for a great harvest of souls. And anyway, who am I
to believe that God would want to reveal anything to me?
These are common inward battles fought by forerunners.
But, when we examine biblical and church history with an
open mind, we see that God often changes history during the
most unlikely circumstances, with the most unlikely people,
in the most unlikely ways – such as an unmarried couple
about to give birth, claiming the pregnancy is from the Holy
Spirit, not man!

A classic biblical example of the tension between the
prophetic and man's own logical understanding is illustrated
in 2 Kings 6, 7. The King of Israel was completely besieged by
the enemies of Israel and trapped in his own city. As if that
were not enough, there had been a major famine in the land
and there was no food in storage. Consequently, barbaric
cannibalism was beginning to take place – mothers were
killing and eating their own children! (2 Kings 6:26–29). At
that time the prophet Elisha spoke to the King saying,
*"Tomorrow about this time a measure of fine flour shall be
sold for a shekel, and two measures of barley for a shekel, in the
gate of Samaria"* (2 Kings 7:1 NASB). In other words he was
prophesying, "Don't worry about all of this. As desperate as
the situation seems God Is Bigger – Trust in Him. He will bring
about a breakthrough that will amaze you and the bread will

be so plentiful it will cost almost nothing!" This was prophecy flying in the face of man's logical perspective; it was a seeming impossibility. The King's right-hand man responded *"Behold, if the* LORD *should make windows in heaven, could this thing be?"* Then Elisha said, *"Behold you shall see it with your own eyes, but you shall not eat of it"* (2 Kings 7:19 NASB).

That very day four men decided in desperation to go over to the camp of their enemies – the Arameans – and seek mercy. They were lepers and so had been cast outside the city walls and were starving. When they arrived however, the Aramean army had completely disappeared! God had caused them to hear the chariots and soldiers of a vast approaching army, so they literally ran, abandoning their entire camp – complete with all of their food supplies. The next day after receiving the good news, the Hebrew people who were starving in captivity stormed the gates of the enemy camp. Elisha's word regarding the provision of inexpensive food in abundance was fulfilled, and the King's right-hand man never did get to eat of it. He was trampled in the gateway as the people stampeded by (2 Kings 7:20). The penalty for his doubting God's ability to "open the heavens" was severe! Similarly, there are, unfortunately, some church leaders today, who arrogantly consider themselves "God's right-hand man". No one can tell them anything because they understand it all. And like some of the Pharisee's in Jesus day, not only do they refuse to enter the gates of the Kingdom, they stand in the way, trying to prevent others from doing so because of their own disbelief that God could be doing a fresh work.

The lepers in this story also illustrate the "forerunner" spirit. It is impossible for a person who has entered into "holy prophetic frustration" to be "filled and satisfied" with the current food available in most churches. It is not so much a reflection on the leadership of the church as it is the hunger for "more" that genuine revelation brings. And as these lepers long ago were stigmatized by the local people, so spiritual forerunners make most within the church feel very uneasy. Like the lepers, forerunner will go to extremes to see their hunger filled. They are not satisfied with the status quo.

Going through the motions of prayer and worship programs just will not suffice.

Finally, one more aspect of the forerunner type needs to be mentioned. There is a tendency, when new waves of God's Spirit moving in the Body of Christ appear, for many Christians to simply "jump on the train". In other words to seek after new experiences, rather than seeking after more of Christ. There are also those who feel they must be seen to be ministering in this new "flow".

To mitigate matters, we are very much living in the information age – a time when what happens in a small obscure meeting one night, can be hyped all over the world by the next morning. With the rapid growth of the Internet, publicity has now become extremely cheap. We have too many preachers, prophetic wannabes and self-labeled revivalists, who, under the guise of "serving God" are, in reality, busy as beavers trying to build and promote their own empires and reputations. Glossy ads and brochures promise the prospective conference attendee "they will get their miracle". As my friend Tommy Tenney says, our tendency is to "hype the stream into a trickle" rather than quietly pray it into a true river of life. Too many preachers can preach for an hour about "their calling to the nations", "their vision", and "their anointing". Meanwhile, Jesus may have been mentioned just once or twice.

The outstanding, fundamental characteristic of a true forerunner however, is they are not nearly so concerned about their own ministry before man as they are about simply seeing Christ Jesus being glorified. In fact, a true forerunner is more interested in *ministering to the person of God* than they are in *ministering before man*. The true forerunner's cry, like John the Baptist's, is not "Make my ministry bigger and more powerful", but "I must decrease, so that He [Jesus] might increase."

The primary trait of a true forerunner is simply a hunger for more of Jesus.

On one occasion, John the Baptist's disciples came to him discouraged. After working so hard for so many years, the crowds were beginning to diminish, as were, no doubt, the offerings. They said to John,

> *"Rabbi, that man who was with you on the other side of the Jordan – the one you testified about – well, he is baptizing, and everyone is going to him."*   (John 3:26 NIV)

Jesus after being baptized by John and fasting for 40 days had begun His ministry. The crowds that had once flocked to John were now going after Jesus. John's response was,

> *"The bride belongs to the bridegroom. The friend who attends the bridegroom waits and listens for him, and is full of joy when he hears the bridegroom's voice. That joy is mine, and it is now complete. He must become greater; I must become less."*   (John 3:29–30 NIV)

John's impetus and fire for ministry was not derived from his ambition or personal agenda. Rather his heart was simply for the voice of the bridegroom to be made known to the bride. John was not motivated by his reputation, ego, finance, or followers.

Today, many ministries play the "promotion game" and so prostitute their gifts and talents. On the throne of their hearts is the king of man – Ego. The least move of the Holy Spirit they are involved in tends to be blown out of all proportion. Instead of delighting in the person of God and His love, their success is determined by the size of the crowd and the significance of the conference.

Chapter 2

Open Heavens (part 1)

"If the Lord should open the floodgates of the heavens,
could this happen?"
(2 Kings 7:2 NIV)

"Be Thou to me a rock of habitation,
to which I may continually come;
Thou hast given commandment to save me,
For Thou art my rock and my fortress."
(Psalm 71:3 NASB)

The "baby" of revival

In February of 1998 I hosted three days of meetings in Fort
Wayne, Indiana for two churches. The first meeting was on a
Sunday morning with both churches combined. The Lord
gave me a phrase to speak on: "The church of the city is
pregnant with revival, but if we don't learn to elevate our
hearts above our heads, our head-knowledge will kill the
baby." I preached the message at both the morning and
evening services.

The next day, the daughter of one of the senior pastors of
the two churches went with her husband and family to the
hospital. Her first baby was overdue by eleven days. After
settling her in, with all the usual monitoring systems in
place, she was given medication to induce labor. Shortly after
that the baby's heartbeat stopped. The staff went into
emergency procedures and a doctor was rushed in. The
doctor told her to get on her knees and put her head down

low. She had to literally "elevate her heart above her head". When she did so, the baby's heartbeat was restored. The doctor then went on to do a cesarean delivery of the baby. The baby was delivered healthy, but they found the umbilical cord was wrapped three times around the neck of the baby. If they had tried to deliver the baby in the normal way, they would have killed him.

Open heavens

We can't go on presuming, through our traditions and head knowledge, that we know precisely what God can do and how He wants to do it. We need a people desperate enough for *open heavens* – that in their cry to see more of God in the land they will "elevate their hearts above their heads"; a people who will ascend the hill of the Lord to seek His face, but also go to the low place of worship and brokenness.

The cost John the Baptist ultimately paid for doing God's will was losing his head, but the chief characteristic of a true forerunner is not their reputation or ministry before man – it is their joy in Him and their cry of "more of Him, and less of me".

Open heavens: what does it mean and can it really happen this side of heaven? The term is used many different times in the Bible. Basically it denotes a time, season, or place, in which there is a great freedom for some on earth to more clearly and powerfully experience God and His reign. It is a time of releasing either God's favor or wrath, for a release of His blessing and/or judgement. But, always it is indicative of a time of exponential increase on the earth of God's power and purposes. In fact, in the first story in which we read of "open heavens" God radically changed all of life on earth. In Genesis 7:11 we read "the floodgates of the heavens were opened". For Noah and his family, although not without difficulty, it released great blessing, while for all others it released judgement and doom. It is helpful to picture those torrential, flooding rains that fell at the first instance of open heavens, because almost always, at least for those involved, open heavens mean a change is coming that, will often dramatically effect the lives of many.

There are several basic stories in the Bible concerning open heavens that we will examine throughout this book. Genesis 28 tells the story of Jacob experiencing open heavens, although we don't actually read that phrase in the story. Instead Jacob uses the term the "gate of God", which is the Hebrew word *sha'ar*, meaning "an opening" as in a door or gate. The basic understanding is of an *opening*, or a *freedom* to experience that which is ordinarily unavailable. In church history during times of great harvest which significantly touched society, the churches involved experienced far more than normal church growth. When one reads accounts of revivals, such as the Welsh Revival which began in 1904, or the Outer Hebrides off the north coast of Scotland in the 1950s, the stories predominantly tell of a great freedom due to the exceptional presence of God's Spirit prior to the move beginning.

Generally speaking, the Bible speaks of three distinct heavens. The third heaven is what the apostle Paul was referring to when he spoke of a man he knew who had been *"caught up to the third heaven"* (2 Corinthians 12:2). The third heaven is where the very throne of God is. It is what we normally refer to as *heaven*. The second heaven is the realm that resides between the third heaven and the physical heavens of our earth, as we know them. The second realm is where the demonic principalities reside. It is for this reason that Satan is referred to as the *"prince of the power of the air, the spirit who is now at work in those who are disobedient"* (Ephesians 2:2 NASB). The first heaven is the realm under man's authority. It is the earth and the sky above us, reaching as far as the furthest rocket can fly or the most powerful telescope can see.

The book of Daniel chapter 10 relates how Daniel had been fasting and praying for three weeks. On the twenty-first day of his fast the angel Gabriel came to him with encouragement, revelation, and wisdom from God. Gabriel explained that Daniel's prayers had been heard on the first day. In fact, Gabriel had been sent by God (from the third heaven) to Daniel immediately. However, the prince of Persia, a demonic prince and fallen angel (in the second heaven) fought Gabriel in an attempt to prevent him reaching Daniel (in the first heaven). It was not until Michael the archangel came to Gabriel's assistance against the prince of Persia that Gabriel was able to break through into our realm (Daniel 10:2–3; 12:13).

In Deuteronomy 28, God warned the people of the serious consequences of disobeying His commandments (Deuteronomy 28:15). Part of God's judgement would be:

> *"The heaven which is over your head shall be bronze, and the earth which is under you, iron."*
> (Deuteronomy 28:23 NASB)

Here we see the opposite of an open heaven caused by man's sin. Sin is Satan's legal domain. Where sin is rampant, the heavens may be as bronze. But when a culture or population that is engaged in major sin, or idolatry, begins to turn and repent, it begins to open the way for God's blessing to come. Throughout the contemporary church scene of North America, the Isles of the United Kingdom, and Europe, church history has been made and shaped by men and women who prophetically knew that somehow God had more for their day and age. Men and women who dared to believe dreams and visions from God. Men and women who preferred to act on those dreams and visions rather than continuing to allow the status quo be their standard.

David and the Ark of the Lord

There is a critical lesson we must learn from King David's initial attempts to bring the Ark of God to the city of Jerusalem, or the City of David as it was called in 2 Samuel chapter 6. Seen especially in the context of this story, we note that David was a man who was passionately in love with the person of God. Many of the songs, or Psalms, that David wrote had to do with his unquenchable love for the person and presence of God. David was a practitioner of looking beyond God's hand of blessing in order to gaze on the glory of God' face.

Most of our prayers tend to have to do with seeking God's hand of blessing. We seek after His provision, His protection,

His deliverance, His anointing, etc. Essentially there is nothing wrong with that. In fact God desires that, as His children we would look to Him to meet all of our needs. The apostle Paul wrote to the church in Philippi,

> *"My God shall supply all your needs according to His riches in glory in Christ Jesus."*   (Philippians 4:19 NASB)

Jesus stated in the Sermon on the Mount,

> *"Therefore do not worry, saying, 'What shall we eat?' or 'What shall we drink?' or 'What shall we wear?' For after all these things the Gentiles seek. For your heavenly Father knows that you need all these things."*
> (Matthew 6:31–32 NKJV)

But when we only seek God's hand of blessing, our prayer life is out of balance. As proper understanding of the Father Heart of God reveals, it is good and proper to seek Him for all of our needs. However, this is too often where we stop. Rather than a means by which we worship and acknowledge God for who He is, we primarily view our prayer as a means of having our personal needs and desires met. Many do go beyond that however, and enter in to the ministry of praying for others. As Ezekiel put it, God is always looking for those who will *"stand in the gap before Me"* (Ezekiel 22:30). But as critical as interceding for the lost and broken, or for governments and political leaders, is, it is still not far enough. If we stop there, then we are still not entering into the heart of prayer-worship that God seeks and desires. David exemplified the prayer-worshipper, and as a result was esteemed by the Lord.

True worship has little in common with much that we casually practice in many contemporary churches. True worship, in both spirit and in truth is far more than merely singing theologically correct songs for a few minutes in order to prepare our hearts for the preaching and teaching. The primary focus of worship in many congregations is to be theologically correct, and/or culturally relevant. What God considers good worship however, and what we often consider good worship can be two very different things. In fact, I am convinced that what we consider a "good" church service and what God considers a "good" church service can be two very different things.

True worship in essence, is to come before the throne of God (in spirit) and give love, thanksgiving, praise, adoration, and blessings to the person of God. True worship can be noisy with celebration or quiet with intimacy. True worship can be weeping with tears of repentance and restoration, or it can be dancing out of a fresh heart-revelation of the awesomeness of God's goodness. For sure, any particular posture of worship such as loud celebration or kneeling in reverence can be made into a religious ritual devoid of any real interaction with the Holy Spirit. However, when we read in the Psalms about worship on earth, or when we examine Daniel's or the apostle John's revelations of worship in heaven, we see many varying expressions of worship taking place except well-behaved, dignified boredom. One suspects that most participants in congregations today realize they are not truly engaging the person of God, otherwise we would not see so many people feeling comfortable with showing up for church services ten minutes after the worship has begun. As long as a consumer mindset grips our view of worship, prayer and church, we will continue to see prayer and worship meetings as merely a means to get more from God, rather than more of God.

As we have noted, King David was a worshipper. In fact, according to the prophet Samuel, that is why God chose David to replace Saul – because David was a man after God's own heart (1 Samuel 13:14). We read in 2 Samuel 6 that David's desire after becoming the King of Israel and Judah was to bring the Ark of God back into the city, years after it had been captured by the Philistines. The Ark, even though it was covered with gold and with a replication of the cherubim carved over it, was essentially just a box. However, God ordained it to symbolize a meeting place with the very Presence of the Lord God Jehovah as the Hebrews traveled through the wilderness. It was placed in the Holy of Holies, in the tent made for it that Moses called "the tent of meeting". Later, after David's day, it was housed in the Holy of Holies of the temple Solomon built.

Exodus 33:8–10 says that when Moses used to go into the tent of meeting and present himself before God, a cloud of God's glory would descend on the tent. When Moses ascended Mt Sinai in Exodus 34 and met with God, the Bible says that his face shone from the meeting. In the same way, a chief characteristic of places and times of open heavens is that God's manifest glory is no longer a theology we believe in, but a reality we experience. Arthur Wallace, the author of the classic book on revival, *Revival: the Rain From Heaven* said,

> "Revival, is more than big meetings and great excitement. It is more than a great harvest of converts. It is more than numbers of Christians being revived and filled with the Spirit. One may have any one of these without revival, and yet revival includes them all."

He, Wallis, maintained the one thing that truly characterized a move of God in revival was nothing less than the manifest glory of God's Presence.

Some would warn at this point, "We must not seek after experiences, rather we must seek after God." I would wholeheartedly agree with that, except that biblically we must recognize two truths about seeking God. First, we are exhorted to seek after the *person of God*, not merely theology or thoughts *about* God. Secondly, there are times, as those men and women whom God used powerfully in the Bible found out, when if even a fraction of the glory of God's Presence is encountered it is not only a real experience, but often one of fearfulness and transformation. We must seek God, not mere experience, but because God is a living, all-powerful being who created us for real relationship, His Presence can and often does bring about life-changing experiences. Our lives must be firmly based on the written word of God. But, just as Jesus lived by and quoted the written Word, He was also led by the Holy Spirit.

Many leaders live in such fear of *experience* that their church's relationship with God resembles a marriage where husband and life simply live in a "platonic relationship". The couple share thoughts, ideas, philosophy (theology), tastes, and culture. But, because they never experience intimacy there are never any children. Those Christian critics of all contemporary Pentecostals' and Charismatics' experience need to remember Jesus' encouragement regarding the Holy Spirit:

> *"And I say to you, ask, and it shall be given to you; seek, and you shall find; knock, and it shall be opened to you. For everyone who asks, receives; and he who seeks, finds; and to him who knocks, it shall be opened. Now suppose one of you fathers is asked by his son for a fish; he will not give him a snake instead of a fish, will he? Or if he is asked for an egg, he will not give him a scorpion, will he? If you then, being evil, know how to give good gifts to your children, how much more shall your heavenly Father give the Holy Spirit to those who ask Him?"*   (Luke 11:9–13 NASB)

We are to seek after God, His gifts and His Spirit – not in fear of Satan's ability to deceive us, but with a confidence in the Father's love for us and His power to lead us by His Spirit and written Word.

David desired the Ark of the Lord and pursued it, not because it was a box of great beauty with gold and intricate carvings, but because He was desperate for the presence of the Lord. In Psalm 27 we read of David's great love for the presence of God. He writes,

> *"One thing I have asked from the LORD, that I shall seek: that I may dwell in the house of the LORD all the days of my life,*
> *To behold the beauty of the LORD, and to meditate in His temple."*   (Psalm 27:4 NASB)

2 Samuel chapter 6 begins the tale of the bringing the Ark of God to the City of David. David started out at Baalah of Judah with 30,000 of his chosen soldiers of the tribe of Judah. He placed the Ark on a new cart and proceeded with intense worship. When they came to the threshing floor of Nacon, the oxen stumbled and nearly upset the Ark. One of David's

men, named Uzza, reached out to steady the Ark and died instantly. David immediately grew angry at the Lord, but also greatly afraid (2 Samuel 6:8–9). It is one thing to pray casually "God, I just want more of you" and to have a revelation of the salvation of God, but it is another thing altogether to experience even a glimpse of the awesome glory of God. It can be one thing to have a revelation of the Lamb of God, and an entirely different thing to experience a revelation of the Lion of the Tribe of Judah!

The apostle Paul wrote to the church in Corinth,

> *"Now the Lord is the Spirit, and where the Spirit of the Lord is, there is freedom. And we, who with unveiled faces all reflect the Lord's glory, are being transformed into his likeness with ever-increasing glory, which comes from the Lord, who is the Spirit."*   (2 Corinthians 3:17–18 NIV)

We can get very used to the comforting theology that our God is omnipresent – a truth that is spoken of throughout Scripture. When we give our lives to Christ, Jesus in the form of His Holy Spirit is always with us and will never leave us nor forsake us. Jesus also told His disciples that whenever two or more of them were gathered in His Name He would also be with them.

We understand from the Bible that God in His vastness is in all places at all times. In Psalm 139:7–12 David stated,

> *"Where can I go from your Spirit?*
> *Where can I flee from your presence?*
> *If I go up to the heavens, you are there;*
> *if I make my bed in the depths, you are there.*
> *If I rise on the wings of the dawn,*
> *if I settle on the far side of the sea,*
> *even there your hand will guide me,*
> *your right hand will hold me fast.*
> *If I say, 'Surely the darkness will hide me*
> *and the light become night around me,'*
> *even the darkness will not be dark to you;*
> *the night will shine like the day,*
> *for darkness is as light to you."*   (NIV)

Such knowledge has greatly comforted many saints especially during times of hardship, or persecution. Yet what David earnestly sought was far more than the promises of God's protection and provision. His heart was hungry for the very *person* of God.

There is an unparalleled freedom of the grace of God that comes from being in His Presence, or at least as much of His presence as we can know in this realm of existence. It has been far too convenient for preachers and Bible teachers to pass off certain biblical promises and experiences as "not for today" or strictly for the sweet "by-and-by". The truth is, too often we're just not hungry enough to *really seek the face of God*. We have allowed ourselves to settle for a "low roof" in our "tents of meeting" with God. In many cases the ceilings are so low that there is simply no room for God to really show up in His glory. At times His hand can reach in and bring blessing, correction, healing, conviction, etc. But to really experience some of what Moses experienced on the mountain of the Lord, or what David was crying out for in Psalm 27, we need to *raise the roof*. We need to raise the canopy of the tent to make room for the glory of His Presence.

In his frustration at the death of Uzza, David had left the Ark nearby at the house of a man named Obed-Edom. Obed-Edom was glad to have the Ark in his home because his chief desire was to be near to the very presence of God. We know from the tabernacle of continuous worship that David established with the Ark, that Obed-Edom went with the Ark to minister before the Lord (1 Chronicles 15:18–21), and 1 Chronicles 15:24 tells us that Obed-Edom served God as one of the Levites playing on a harp. But he also served as a doorman, or gatekeeper for the Ark. Obed-Edom realized experientially what we often only sing about in our worship services:

> *"Better is one day in your courts*
> *than a thousand elsewhere;*
> *I would rather be a doorkeeper in the house of my God*
> *than dwell in the tents of the wicked."*

(Psalm 84:2 NIV)

Raising the roof

I have been in many corporate meetings in the last few years that were primarily characterized by worship and waiting on God – where there have been healings, miracles, deliverances, repentance, people saved – all without any pulpit ministry (at least by man). At one meeting I attended in Baltimore in the spring of 1998, a woman approached the front crying out loudly. We had been worshipping the Lord for about 90 minutes when she came forward. She was not only very disturbed herself, but also very disturbing to the rest of the crowd who were intently focused on God. We found out that the reason for her outburst was that she had been completely healed after being paralyzed for 17 years. Seventeen years previously she had a brain tumor removed and damage caused by the operation resulted in paralysis in her left arm, hand, and shoulder. In an instant, during the time of worship, everything, including the atrophied muscles, were restored. Later her doctor, who she had been seeing for over 10 years, pronounced it a miracle. Obviously, the Bible encourages us to pray and to lay hands on the sick in prayer, but when God really shows up, as Obed-Edom experienced, many things change for the better just because He is there.

We read in Acts 5:15 of people bringing the sick into the streets and laying them on beds and mats so that *"at least Peter's shadow might fall on some of them as he passed by."* If, as that verse suggests, on occasion some were being healed when Peter's shadow fell on them, the question needs to be asked, "What was really happening?" I vividly remember that question coming up in a seminary class covering the book of Acts and the Pauline Epistles. The seminary firmly believed in the inerrancy of the Scriptures. But as we read over that passage one of the students, who was already functioning as a pastor in a church, asked with great skepticism in his voice, "Come on, what's this all about!" Many of us in that school, even though we firmly believed, at least theologically, that the Bible was completely true, felt that surely something must be wrong with this account, because Peter's experiences were so far removed from our own. Was Peter's shadow actually healing anyone? The answer is, no –

it was the shadow of the One in whom Peter had hidden (Psalm 17:8).

So, how can we raise our expectations of what God can do? How do we "raise the roof" of our own "tents of meeting"? Again, we can look to the Ark to teach us. The Ark had cherubim made of hammered gold positioned over it. The cherubim began on either end of the ark and rose over it to meet in the middle with their wings outspread. They were intended to be a replica of the cherubim who attend God's presence to remind the Levites how close to His presence they were. The Bible tells us that cherubim surround the very throne of God in continual worship. Isaiah chapter 6 gives us an insight into these mysteries as we read of Isaiah's revelation of the throne room of God. He saw seraphs hovering above the Lord who was seated on His throne. Each of the worshipping angels had six wings. With two they covered their faces, with two they covered their feet, and with two they flew, or hovered. Isaiah records in verse three that *"they were calling to one another: 'Holy, holy, holy is the* LORD *Almighty; the whole earth is full of his glory.'"* These worshipping beings are effectively a living canopy, or the roof of the tent over the throne of God. Similarly they "covered" the Ark of God's presence.

We can raise the roof of our tents of meeting by simply being biblical (John 4:24). That is to say by focusing on worshipping the Father *in Spirit and in truth*. Psalm 22:3 in the King James version says of God,

"Thou art holy, O thou that inhabitest the praises of Israel."

When we really press in with all of our hearts, with a desperation for Him, our worship, adoration, and reverence becomes on earth what the Seraph do in heaven. We do in reality what the beaten cherubs over the box do in simulation – we form a canopy of praise! As we boldly, by the grace of the cross *"approach the throne of grace with confidence"* (Hebrews 4:16 NIV), we can raise the roof of the tent higher and higher and actually make room for His Presence.

Of course, I am speaking symbolically. But, even Solomon, on the day of dedication of his magnificent and costly monument to God acknowledged, *"Will God really dwell on earth? The heavens, even the highest heaven, cannot contain you. How much less this temple I have built!"* God, in His awesomeness and majesty can no more be confined, or housed, by anything man can make than an elephant squeezed through the eye of a needle. However, because God's love is as powerful as His glory, He chooses to dwell among men as well as in Heaven. Indeed, because of His great love for us He chooses to place His Spirit actually within our very hearts when we surrender our lives to Jesus as our Lord and Savior.

David's mistake in his first attempt to bring home the Ark was to have placed it on a cart drawn by oxen. We can imagine that this cart was, most probably, an extremely elaborate one. 2 Samuel 6:3 states that David had his men get a "new cart ready". Most likely, it was specifically made to bring up the glory of God. Therein lay the problem.

The actual base of the Ark had two rings on either side. The rings were placed there so that two poles might be inserted through the rings and men might carry the Ark without touching it. It was never God's intention that His Presence be carried by anything other than living beings. Here also lies a problem for many contemporary churches and leaders.

It is very common for pastors and church leaders to spend thousands of dollars every year to attend church growth seminars so that they might learn the latest methodology, or programs that have worked for another leader in another part of the world. And often it is helpful to learn from another's successes and failures. But the Holy Spirit will not and cannot be reduced to mere programs or methods. God's Presence and anointing does not so much rest on strategies and programs as it does on people.

For the last ten years or so, an area of church growth that has been widely explored is that of "seeker-sensitive" churches. The central premise is that, because there are so many people under the age of forty with no prior experience of church, the church needs to lower the entry threshold for the average person – making it more relevant and accessible as much as possible.

Often this means focusing on certain worship and speaking styles that make the visitor feel comfortable rather than challenged. For some pastors of "seeker-sensitive" or "user-friendly" churches, the cross, denying oneself, repentance, or the blood of the lamb, would not be heavily emphasized during Sunday meetings. The underlying idea is to get people into the church first, then to belong to the Lord, which in itself is not bad thinking. To be sure, many churches are caught up in a "religious culture" that is hard for the average non-churchgoer to relate to. Many congregations have made an idol out of a particular style of music that was popular decades ago and now are a complete turn-off to the unsaved. The question is, however, how many leaders have been as concerned about seeking and being sensitive to the Holy Spirit as they are concerned with being sensitive to people? We have many *user-friendly churches*, but what about some *Uzza-friendly churches*! Churches that have sought to make a resting place (Isaiah 66:1–2) for God by learning to minister to God through prayer and worship.

I have found that when it comes to the choice of making people comfortable or God comfortable, it is not necessarily an either/or scenario. That is to say, even non-Christians when they experience a church service where God is really present, are often more cognizant of His presence than Christians who are primarily focused on the traditional program or agenda. The question also needs to be asked, "When someone is saved at a contemporary seeker-sensitive church, what are they being saved into?" A religious system built for man, or into a family who are adamantly in love with God? Jesus stated *"My house shall be called a house of prayer, but you are making it a robbers den"* (Matthew 21:13 NASB). Are churches that are almost exclusively geared towards making man comfortable robbing both God and the people of the intimacy the Great Commandment calls for? How does the seeker mentality reconcile with the Father's desire to have people who will *"worship in Spirit and in truth"* (John 4:23 NASB).

One of the dumbest thoughts any church (or even secular) leader can have is to believe that they will somehow see different results despite continuing to do things exactly as they have always done them. If good preaching, relevant programs, and great singing were going to win the world for

Christ, then it would have been won a long time ago! We need leaders in the Body of Christ today who will spend at least as much time praying and waiting on the Spirit of God as they do studying church growth techniques.

The initial harvest that began on the day of Pentecost cannot be attributed to anything more than the Holy Spirit and a group of desperate men and women that were willing to seek God. But, the question arises, "Isn't simply praying ... too simple?" Isaiah was so profoundly correct when he wrote on behalf of the Lord,

> *"'For my thoughts are not your thoughts, neither are your ways my ways,' declares the* LORD. *'As the heavens are higher than the earth, so are my ways higher than your ways and my thoughts than your thoughts.'"* (Isaiah 55:8)

To spend a lot of time in prayer, waiting on God, and merely worshipping Him may seem a waste of time to many. Just as to many it seemed wasteful when the woman poured out costly perfume on the feet of Jesus. The truth is however, that it is humbling to cry out to God. It is humbling to spend time just waiting on His Presence. It is humbling to say to oneself; "The very best I can do today is to minister to He who is best of all". It appeals to our pride to "build new and extravagant carts". It proves to our flesh that we're really doing something when we make great sacrifices. But, as David learned, the true sacrifice that God is after is *"a broken and contrite heart"* (Psalm 51:17 NASB). Prayer by very nature, repels the proud, because in essence, to seriously pray is to recognize that what we need the most, only God can provide.

· *Chapter 3*

Open Heavens (part 2)

"I'm coming back to the heart of worship,
and it's all about You, ...
I'm sorry Lord for the thing I've made it,
when it's all about You,
all about You, Jesus."
(Matt Redman, *The Heart of Worship*)

The awesomeness of God

Once while speaking to a group of leaders of a certain
century-old denomination in Europe, I focused for a few
moments on the awesomeness of God. After the meeting one
of the priests privately rebuked me saying I should not speak
about the awesomeness of God because that is not how God
wants people to look on Him as such. He continued to say we
should merely focus on the quiet goodness of God. That
priest, although probably well-meaning, failed to see the
connection between the compromise with sin, such as
homosexuality, that his denomination has made and the
lack of a fuller, biblical, revelation of God. For over a century
now his denomination had been more influenced by the
values and mores of the world than it has been an influence
on it. We need a people to arise today and seek God through
prayer and worship in the Holy Spirit, but also *in truth* – in
other words, as He truly is! Much of the world's population is
crying out for a true revelation of spiritual reality. Church

leaders today need to freshly realize that they can either fear God, or fear man, but not both.

The question that needs to be asked in the church today is, "How much of God do we really want?" When Jacob experienced the *sha'ar*, or "open gate" of God, he encountered God's presence in a way he never had previously.

> *"When Jacob awoke from his sleep, he thought, 'Surely the* Lord *is in this place, and I was not aware of it.' He was afraid and said, 'How awesome is this place! This is none other than the house of God; this is the gate of heaven.'"*
> (Genesis 28:16–17 NIV)

On several occasions, both in private prayer meetings and in larger corporate settings, when I have experienced even a little of God's awesome power and holiness, I have been filled with a great fear. Not a fear that would cause one to run from God, quite the contrary – a fear that causes one to want to bring every area, thought, dream, hope, practice, and breath, under the Lordship of Jesus.

A true love of Jesus must grow to include a revelation of His awesome power and holiness or else it is an immature love. Just as in a healthy marriage, there must be more than merely a sharing of ideas and culture. The deep intimacy that should characterize every marriage makes that relationship sacred. If it is missing, the marriage will not bear fruit. There tends to be a clinging to shallow love among much of the church – a "so-called" love for God, but without any fear of God. The fact is, the Bible has as many promises for those who *fear the Lord* as there are for those who *love the Lord*. Proverbs 22:4 for example reads,

> *"Humility and the fear of the* Lord
> *bring wealth and honor and life."* (NIV)

After speaking at a conference a few years ago, an individual approached me with a question. He quoted what Jesus stated in John 15 regarding abiding in Him, with the accompanying promise that if we did so we would bear much fruit. He was criticizing my message because it appeared to him I was saying that our walk with God should be *more than* simply "abiding". I told him I agreed with his statement, but pointed out that our "abiding in Christ" needed to include worshipping the Father with all of our heart (Mark 12:30), and working our salvation out with "fear and trembling", because it is the Spirit of the living God who lives within to "perform His will and good pleasure" (Philippians 2:12). Just as David grew afraid of God when Uzza touched His presence at the threshing floor, so Jacob also became afraid of the Presence of God (Genesis 28:17).

A true fear of God, causes one to so deeply appreciate the compassion, mercy and love of God, that we begin to detest the thought of disappointing or grieving Him. We begin to ardently pursue His will and purposes out of love rather than duty, or prudence. The Psalmist sang,

> *"I run in the path of your commands,*
> *for you have set my heart free."*   (Psalm 119:32 NIV)

Likewise, the prophet Isaiah, when he was caught up into the very throne room of God, was afraid and very aware of his own fragility in comparison to the awesome presence of God. In Isaiah 6 he relates,

> *" 'Woe to me!' I cried. 'I am ruined! For I am a man of unclean lips, and I live among a people of unclean lips, and my eyes have seen the King, the LORD Almighty.' Then one of the seraphs flew to me with a live coal in his hand, which he had taken with tongs from the altar. With it he touched my mouth and said, 'See, this has touched your lips; your guilt is taken away and your sin atoned for.' Then I heard the voice of the LORD saying, 'Whom shall I send? And who will go for us?' And I said, 'Here am I. Send me!' "*
> (Isaiah 6:5–8 NIV)

Isaiah's experience of the awesome glory of God reveals two basic heart responses that are very common among those who gaze upon God. First, he proclaims, *"I am ruined"*. His posture before God, whatever it was before, is now one of deep, profound humility as well as reverential fear. Secondly, when he sees the opportunity to serve God, he proclaims, *"Here am I. Send me!"* His will has been completely captured by the glory of God's being.

The great "I AM"

Throughout Scripture, God refers to Himself as "I AM". The Lord uses this phrase as perhaps the only way He can explain to us what He is really like, as He did when He revealed Himself to Moses in the burning bush. Until we have a revelation of God as the "I AM" though, we tend to focus on ourselves as the "I am". When Isaiah came before the fire of God's Presence he twice identified himself using the phrase "I am", or "Here am I". Until an individual really sees himself in the light of God's Presence he, or she, will usually be the great "I am" of their life, despite their theology. But, just like the day I caught a mere glimpse of the true *I AM* in the hills of San Diego, once the Lord, the great *I AM* reveals Himself to you, your perspective is changed forever.

When you read testimonies of conversions during times of the great historic revivals such as with Finney and others, oftentimes the process of coming to Christ involved episodes of great fear and weeping. Those reactions were not so much due to the great oratory skills of the preachers, but rather just a bit of the presence of the great *I AM*. They were, in fact, experiencing *open heavens*.

Whenever open heavens are truly experienced, worship is the natural response. One can read in Daniel's and John's revelation of the throne of God, of continual worship taking place. David, the man whose heart was after God's, established a tabernacle of continual worship before the Lord's Presence (1 Chronicles 16:40). When Jacob realized that he was in the "gateway" to the very house, or presence of God, he also built an altar of worship there and named the place "Bethel" or "house of God".

When Jesus said *"My house shall be called a house of prayer"* (Matthew 21:13 NASB), He was saying that the place He would inhabit would have to be a place of communion and communication – a place of true intimacy between God and man, not merely a place of religious ritual. At the time Jesus said that, He was in the process of wreaking havoc at the temple. The preceding verse reads,

> *"Jesus entered the temple area and drove out all who were buying and selling there. He overturned the tables of the money changers and the benches of those selling doves."*

In His righteous anger He was overturning the order of man to restore true worship to the Father.

Millions of Christians all over the world have heard of the "Toronto Blessing", as the English Press dubbed it. The term refers to a move of the Holy Spirit that began on the third weekend of January at the Toronto Airport Christian Fellowship and has continued to this day. At the time of writing over 5 million Christians have traveled from almost every country on the face of the earth to Toronto seeking to experience in a new way God's love and refreshment. In May of 1992 while speaking at a prophetic seminar in Toronto, God gave me an open vision of Niagara Falls coming over the city of Toronto. The Lord said that in winter of 1993/94 a move would begin that would go to all the Nations. That prophecy has been well-documented. I preached it several times in Toronto prior to the move actually taking place in the January of 1994. Dr Guy Chevreau printed the bulk of it in his best-selling book *Catch the Fire*. As it happened I was in Europe ministering when the move broke out. My wife let me know that our senior pastor, John Arnott, was wanting to get hold of me on the phone. When I connected with John he told me that "It was all happening"! I asked "What's all happening?" He responded, "What you prophesied is beginning to take place and Christians from churches all over Toronto are coming to our church. We are having meetings every night in order to accommodate everyone."

When I finally did get back to Toronto some week and a half later, I was anxious to attend one of the meetings. The first night I went there were some 900 people present from many different churches, including different denominations.

Our church was only about 350 people strong and it was incredible to see all these people from Anglican, Baptist and Pentecostal congregations coming to our meeting. What blew me away about the meeting however, was not the manifestations of people being powerfully and wonderfully touched by God. Neither was it the crowd that was exciting. To me it was the fact that for the first 90 minutes, a crowd of many different ages, cultures and denominational backgrounds were joyfully and passionately worshipping God with a real fervency and passion. More than anything else this is what connected with my heart.

Worship and prayer are the true barometer of where the church is at. The great English Bible teacher and preacher of the last century, Spurgeon stated,

> "You can tell how popular the church is by the attendance on Sunday morning. You can tell how popular the speaker is by the attendance on Sunday night. But, you can tell how popular Jesus is by the attendance at the prayer meeting."

Consumer church

The truth is we have been consumer oriented in our thinking about most of our church meetings. We have been primarily concerned about what are we going to get out of the meeting. If we are really ever going to get open heavens and establish a *resting place*, rather than a *work place* for the Holy Spirit, we are going to have to move much deeper into true worship. In fact, we don't so much need to *practice* true worship, but become a *people* of true worship. Matt Redman, the worship leader/singer-songwriter from England wrote these lines in his song *The Heart of Worship*:

> "I'm coming back to the heart of worship,
> and it's all about You,
> all about You Jesus.
> I'm sorry Lord for the thing I've made it,
> when it's all about You,
> all about You, Jesus".

We've made church services into so many things. We have become like Jesus' friend Martha who was continually doing the "things of God".

> *" 'You are worried and upset about many things,' Jesus said to her, 'but only one thing is needed. Mary has chosen what is better, and it will not be taken away from her.' "*
> (Luke 10:41–42)

What Mary was guilty of in the eyes of Martha was giving devotion and adoration to Jesus when there was more serious work to be done! Yet the worship of God, in Spirit and truth, is the be all and end all of the Kingdom of God. Until we begin to be practitioners of John 4:24 and not just believers of the Scriptures, at best we will only experience visitations from the Holy Spirit in the corporate church. What we desperately need in our cities today is far more than one or two churches experiencing visitations. We need to establish habitations, or places of open heavens. We need congregations and, really, the church of the city to rise up and become "Bethels" – places where God can be found.

Reaching a "certain" place

While examining Jacob's experience of open heavens there is another aspect that we need to focus on. Jacob arrived in this place called Luz which he later renamed Bethel. It says in Genesis 28:11 that while he was journeying to Haran *"he reached a certain place"*. The King James translation however, uses the word "lighted" – *"he lighted upon a certain place"*. In this passage the King James Version language helps give some critical understanding of open heavens.

The word "lighted" is the Hebrew word *paga* which is often used in the Old Testament in the context of interceding, or intercessory prayer.[1] The basic meaning of the word is to "meet" or "come between". Every now and again in our journey towards the fullness of God's promises, like Jacob we reach or "light upon a certain place". This is the place of open heavens

Whenever we read of men and women whom God has used in a significant way to touch their time and culture with God's love and power, there is always the process of "lighting on a certain place" – a place where all of humanity is on one side and the glory of God and His purposes are on the other. A place of standing in the gap, coming between – the place of the intercessor. For Joshua it was outside the city of Jericho meeting the angel of the Lord (Joshua 5:13–15); for Gideon it was at the altar as he offered up his sacrifice before the angel of the Lord and God consumed it (Judges 6:22); for Moses it was ascending the mountain and beholding the angel of the Lord in the midst of the fire of the burning bush (Exodus 3:2); For Peter, James and John it was when they ascended the mountain and saw Jesus in His glory (Matthew 17:6).

The cycle of revival usually begins with a people who cannot stand to live any longer with the status quo of spirituality that most of the church is content with. A heart cry begins to rise up as, at least a few believers cry out to God with all their hearts for "more"! More than their eyes have ever seen, more than their ears have ever heard. They enter into that which we discussed in Chapter 1 – "Holy Prophetic Frustration". Then somewhere on the journey between their own Beersheba (a pit of death) and Haran (the hills of promotion), they light upon God's glory.

Paul in his second letter to the church in Corinth stated that,

"Where the Spirit of the Lord is, there is freedom."
(2 Corinthians 3:17 NIV)

The timeless question facing the people of God is: "How much of God can we have in this realm?" God's answer is always the same. If we are willing to really seek His face, He desires to fill us so that streams of living water flow out of our innermost beings. The prophet Jeremiah encouraged the exiles in Babylon to not let the fact that they were in captivity breed hopelessness. He stated concerning God's love and blessings *"You will seek me and find me when you seek me with all your heart."* God honors those who are desperately seeking Him. James in the New Testament expressed the same thought this way:

"Submit yourselves, then, to God. Resist the devil, and he will flee from you. Come near to God and he will come near to you. Wash your hands, you sinners, and purify your hearts, you double-minded. Grieve, mourn and wail. Change your laughter to mourning and your joy to gloom. Humble yourselves before the Lord, and he will lift you up."

(James 4:7–10 NIV)

Contradicting this attitude of desperate seeking after God however, is a pharisaical attitude that pervades much of the church. The ethos of the Pharisees today, just as it was in Jesus' day; is "Just be content and don't rock the boat". The call of the Spirit however, is "Abba, Father" – a passionate heartcry for much more of God than any system or program can provide! It is the voice of one crying in the wilderness of church mediocrity.

God never despises a heart hungry for Him. We, like Jacob, can come to a place of great freedom in God. We may feel that we are currently in a place or time that does not appear in any way special or significant. In fact, like Jacob, we can be in a place of deep loneliness and despair. But all of a sudden there is a great freedom in that place because of God's manifest Presence and glory.

The old church building where the Welsh Revival began with the young man Evan Roberts was certainly no place special, in and of itself. Likewise the small building that housed a small, racially mixed congregation at Azusa, Los Angeles was no place special. But, as Paul stated in 2 Corinthians 3:17, *"Where the Spirit of the Lord is, there is Liberty"* (NASB). Because the Presence of God is so much greater in places of open heavens, the corresponding freedom for His love, grace, and power to flow is also exponentially greater The place in and of itself is usually not very significant, but the One who finds a resting place there makes it significant. As Paul continues to say in 2 Corinthians 3, we no longer move so much from blessing to blessing, but rather from glory to glory. And that glory tends to be transforming as it was with Gideon, Moses and the apostles on the day of Pentecost!

What Jacob was actually doing when He came into God's awesomeness is also significant. He was sleeping! He was at rest. Too many times when we begin to seriously pursue the visions and dreams God has given us, we fall into the "cross plus syndrome". The cross plus syndrome occurs when a Christian, or a group of Christians in pursuit of the things of God, forgets the essential grace of the Cross. One begins to think that we need to earn or prove something in order to win God's favor and blessings. What some refer to as "toxic faith" or "spiritual abuse", is the cross plus syndrome. It overtakes a leader's understanding of how God works through the church. It causes us to fall back into religious thinking – that we can somehow earn, or achieve, the things of God apart from His pure grace. Yet Jacob was resting! Psalm 46:10 states,

"Be still, and know that I am God;
I will be exalted among the nations,
I will be exalted in the earth."   (NKJV)

I am not suggesting that we remain purely passive. For sure, faith without works is a dead faith (James 2:26). Jacob had faith and he was also on a journey. He was seeking. But, at a time of rest he experienced a visitation of God in His awesomeness.

A few years ago I was invited to speak at a prophetic conference held in Kansas City by the Kansas City Metro Church led by Mike Bickle. I was to speak at the Saturday sessions. I had been asked by Mike to speak to his church that Sunday morning as well. Mike believed God had spoken to him in a dream that I was going to have a prophetic word for the church.

It was one thing to speak on the topic of prophecy, but quite another to give a prophetic word to that particular church. God has used the Kansas City Metro Church as a fresh stream in the last 15 years to help both rebirth and restore the ministry of the prophetic and the office of the prophet and prophetic ministry in general. Internationally the church, while not without critics or controversy, has a great reputation for being a source of encouragement, revelation, and teaching for the Body of Christ..

The two main sessions on the Saturday which I spoke and ministered at went fine. I ended up being tied up in private meetings until late at night as well. I returned to my hotel room after midnight feeling very tired. I was determined however, to spend as much time as necessary, even if it took all night to wait on the Lord to hear precisely what He wanted me to say to the church the next morning. I couldn't go before any church, but especially that one, without clearly hearing from the Lord if I was truly going to minister prophetically. It's one thing to be prophetic, it's another to be pathetic!

As I began to wait on the Lord and worship Him I read Psalm 127. It was part of my scheduled Bible reading for that day. I often begin my devotions to the Lord by reading a different Psalm. All of a sudden verse 2 jumped out at me. It reads:

"In vain you rise early and stay up late,
toiling for food to eat – for he grants sleep to those he
loves."

As clear as the noon-day sun on a summer's day the Lord was saying to me, "All good and perfect gifts come from Me" (James 1:17). "Revelation belongs to Me and it cannot be earned or purchased. I give it to My friends because I love them". I immediately felt the burden lift off me to "come up with something from God". After worshipping the Lord a bit more I went to bed. When I awoke the next morning after spending some time worshipping the Lord, shaving, showering and dressing, I was picked up by one of the church leaders. During the worship at the first service the Lord gave me four distinct and short "words" for the church based on four very different and seemingly unrelated Bible passages. Although I had no idea, every one of these passages was distinctly significant to the church and the leadership. God was confirming to them things they had long had on their hearts.

I could have stayed up all night trying to "earn something from God". But, even as we are saved by grace alone, so grace is the means by which God continually deals with His children. No matter how mature we think we are, or how far we may have come in our journey, God always looks on us as His children and He expects us to have a childlike faith in His goodness. The call on us is to seek God with all of our hearts, trusting in faith in His inherent goodness, grace, and mercy. That may include "running" to do His will. But, as any long-distance runner will tell you, the muscles and the heart work best when the runner is relaxed and not striving. God met with Jacob at a moment when he was in total rest. All the religious striving in the world is not going to force God to do anything. The only thing that we can do to really move God is to let our hearts be broken. That is the one thing on our part that can impress God.

> *"Thus says the LORD, 'Heaven is My throne, and the earth is My footstool. Where then is a house you could build for Me? And where is a place that I may rest? For My hand made all these things, thus all these things came into being,' declares the LORD. 'But to this one I will look, to him who is humble and contrite of spirit, and who trembles at My word.'"*
>
> (Isaiah 66:1–2 NASB)

Note

1. See Isaiah 53:12; 59:16; Jeremiah 7:16; 27:18; 36:25.

Chapter 4

The Power of Brokenness (part 1)

Probably the most vital ingredients of a person who truly desires an encounter with the awesome presence of God are humility and transparency. One who possesses those qualities is well positioned to connect with God's open heavens. Unfortunately for us, these qualities are most often honed with the tool of brokenness.

Brokenness! The word conjures up images of things ready for the rubbish heap. It brings to mind the exact opposite of brand new things in nice stores, shops and showrooms. The word "brokenness" is the antithesis of the new and shiny condition that we like things in life to possess – especially in our western culture that places such a high premium on youth and newness. Yesterday's hot item is today's throw away.

I remember the first time I heard a Christian voice the phrase "The way God treats His friends, He's lucky He has any at all." I was shocked that anyone who loved God would say that. Especially as the one saying it was a good friend I was working with in ministry. It took more than a few moments for me to get past my religious, plastic, superficial thoughts about God and His love. Because the truth be known, the route God ordains us to walk on our journey towards wholeness always includes embracing the cross. And to embrace the cross means to step over the threshold of our natural abhorrence of discomfort.

God's ways and thoughts are completely contrary to humanity's. In our thinking to be as complete, or perfect, as possible includes avoiding pain, loneliness and suffering at all costs. For sure God's desire is to bring us into wholeness and abundant life. But, the route God ordains for us to come into His wholeness can sometimes appear completely contrary to that goal of wholeness.

It seems that we human beings fall endlessly into the trap of feeling wise and all-knowing. Just when we get to that point, God often pulls the rug out from underneath us. In fact, when we are feeling smug in our imagined state of wisdom, God does far more than pull out the rug – sometimes He pushes us over the edge of a cliff. Of course, He provides us with a parachute, but it is usually quite unappealing – His grace and mercy; a complete childlike dependency on Him.

Human beings are so adept at making positive confessions that we can get to the point where we deceive ourselves about our true standing with God. When He desires to shake us back into reality we usually find it convenient to label those palpable flips and fireballs as "spiritual warfare" – in other words we pass it off as the work of the devil. Those that consider all difficulties and trials in life as merely the work of the devil and something that can instantly be warded off by a rebuke or a quick prayer have failed to take the book of Job into any sort of theological consideration. And it really is amazing how when trouble hits, some are quick to forget that God is all-powerful and amazingly good! The apostles of the early church, unlike many leaders today, drew both faith and comfort from the fact that when persecution began in earnest against them, that not only was God still in control, but that He even at times predestined those attacks (Acts 4:28).

As the Lord said through Isaiah,

"As the heavens are higher than the earth,
So are My ways higher than your ways,
And My thoughts than your thoughts."

(Isaiah 55:9 NKJV)

In fact, not only are our ways so completely different from God's, but God delights in working in ways that appear simple, or foolish, to our understanding. The apostle Paul stated it this way to the church of Corinth:

> *"For since in the wisdom of God the world through its wisdom did not know him, God was pleased through the foolishness of what was preached to save those who believe."*
> (1 Corinthians 1:21 NIV)

And again,

> *"For the foolishness of God is wiser than man's wisdom, and the weakness of God is stronger than man's strength."*
> (1 Corinthians 1:25 NIV)

The chief example as Paul wrote in his letter was Jesus, the Messiah, crucified as the worst sort of criminal of the day. That made no sense whatsoever to either the Jews or Gentiles of that time. In fact, it makes no sense in our day either. How can one say that "God is love" when He allowed His only begotten Son to suffer and die the way He did?

The picture of Jesus crucified is the ultimate picture of God working in ways so confounding to human logic. Throughout the Bible however, we find this principle appearing consistently. Such as God using Rahab, the prostitute, to protect two Hebrew spies and open up a whole city to the Hebrew Army (Joshua 2:1); or God telling Abraham that he would be the "father of many nations" when he was 99 years of age. He and his wife were not only long past childbearing age, as yet they had been completely unable to conceive any children (Genesis 17:4).

Simply put, God has ordained brokenness and the cross as the path we must take to maturity, while our overwhelmingly natural leanings are towards a pain-free journey complete with parades and banners.

Biblical perfection

At this point, it's probably necessary to cover some basic semantics. First off, it is God's desire that we pursue wholeness. Jesus said,

"Be perfect, therefore, as your heavenly Father is perfect."
(Matthew 5:48 NIV)

Paul wrote to the church in Colosse,

"We proclaim him, admonishing and teaching everyone with all wisdom, so that we may present everyone perfect in Christ." (Colossians 1:28 NIV)

The word in the original New Testament language we translate as "perfect" is *teleioo*.[1] It does not have quite the same meaning as is commonly used in modern English which is taken to mean completely 100% without flaw. Rather, the Greek word means to become complete, fulfilled, finished and consecrated. The difference between the two definitions is subtle but important. If we think of the perfection that Jesus said we should aim for from a modern English understanding than the task is hopeless. How can we even begin to think of ourselves as being "perfect" – never making a mistakes or committing any sin whatsoever, ever again? But, if we understand that the Father's goal for us is to become "whole" – healthy and functioning completely in our relationships with Him and one another, then we understand that the goal is one of *quality of life* rather than legalistic perfection. Therein, lies the key to understanding why God's path to wholeness sometimes involves a breaking process which, in our thinking, is counterproductive.

When a surgeon has a patient with confirmed cancer on the operating table he proceeds to cut into the body of the patient. In most situations taking a knife and piercing another's body would be an act of violence. But, when a surgeon does it is understood as an *operation* that will hopefully bring healing to the patient, so that they might become whole. The operation itself can be very serious and is often traumatic. And, when God operates on us, we are not usually anaesthetized like on the operating table! We are very aware of the hurt, trauma and stress we are going through. But, much like an operation, if the cancer is not dealt with and we walk away from the process prematurely, we continue in our diseased state as before.

The problem with the process of brokenness is that . . . well, it's painful! There can be a shattering of dreams, vision, ambition and self-perception. Often though, that is God's very goal and the reason why He allows us to become broken. He needs to wake us up to the cancers of hurt, anger, pride, envy, etc., that lie within our hearts and souls. In our illusions of health and wisdom we are usually merrily on our way, thinking that we have everything together, and are at least slightly better than everyone else around us. The Bible refers to that as *pride*. Jeremiah said,

> *"The heart is deceitful above all things and desperately wicked; who can know it?"*   (Jeremiah 17:9 NKJV)

We often despair of going through times of disillusionment, but the upside is that we get rid of our illusions concerning ourselves. Those illusions are quite often the greatest barriers to healthy relationships among friends, associates, church, family, and marriage. We can be so eager to remove the splinter from another's eyes that we fail to realize our perceptions are way off, due to the log in our own eyes. As the saying goes "hurting people hurt people". Due to false perceptions of self, too many of us go through life critically aware of others' shortcomings, never realizing that not only do we have the same problem, but that our problems are exacerbating the problems in others! After all, it's usually the people who have the same hang-up as ourselves who annoy us the most!

The prophet Jeremiah was a man who had God's heart for the wholeness of Israel. He is sometimes referred to as "the weeping prophet" because of the lamentations of his soul for Israel. He longed that they would become all that they could be in God's love. In Jeremiah 18:2–6 we find this parable.

> *" 'Arise and go down to the potter's house, and there I shall announce My words to you.' Then I went down to the potter's house, and there he was, making something on the wheel. But the vessel that he was making of clay was spoiled in the hand of the potter; so he remade it into another vessel, as it pleased the potter to make. Then the word of the LORD came*

to me saying, 'Can I not, O house of Israel, deal with you as this potter does?' declares the Lord. *'Behold, like the clay in the potter's hand, so are you in My hand, O house of Israel'"*
(NASB)

Blessing and breaking

There is an appropriate saying that transcends the apparent dichotomy between God's desire for wholeness in His children and His willingness to break us: "God loves us just the way we are, but He loves us too much to leave us the way we are". God, in His grand and awesome love for each one of us is too committed to our wellbeing for us to really understand. Much like a child being disciplined, it can be very hard to perceive the discipline as possibly being good at that particular moment.

Most people feel a need to constantly be in control of their lives. In the light of this God will sometimes allow events, indeed series of events, to effectively shatter our confidence in our abilities to control and regulate our lives. The Psalmist wrote,

"Though you have made me see troubles, many and bitter,
  you will restore my life again;
from the depths of the earth
  you will again bring me up.
You will increase my honor
  and comfort me once again."   (Psalm 71:20–21 NIV)

Here the worshipper, perhaps David, from a posture of thanksgiving and love, is acknowledging this frustrating dichotomy – that God loves us so deeply, yet is willing to allow us times of pain and frustration.

The Eastern mindset is much more comfortable with such apparent contradictions than the western. Paul stated that the Jewish people sought after signs, or indicators, while the Greeks looked for wisdom. Those of us with a western world mindset find it very hard to accept that not everything is black and white. We love our systems, programs and convenient answers. The church of the west finds it too convenient to dismiss as "not for today" that which cannot be completely perceived from a rational understanding. Our problem with God is that not only is His wisdom far above ours, but He moves and speaks with mankind in ways that are *trans-rational*. That is to say, He is spirit and the language and work of the Holy Spirit often bypasses the mind and goes directly to the heart. A head knowledge of God is one thing – a heart knowledge another. It takes both to really be a disciple of Christ and a friend of God. Additionally, God is love and His love totally transcends any and all of our standards of love, sacrifice and giving.

The classic example is God – the giver of rich and extravagant love, allowing His precious Son – Jesus, the Lamb of God – to suffer for us. The picture of Jesus suffering on the cross is familiar the whole world over, even to non-Christians. As well, all believers and many non-believers are familiar with the verse that sums up the entire gospel:

> *"For God so loved the world that he gave his one and only Son, that whoever believes in him shall not perish but have eternal life."* (John 3:16 NIV)

But how many have considered John 3.16 from the perspective of the Father's incredible love for His only begotten son? What human father would allow their own son to be beaten, tortured, ridiculed, mocked and then publicly and with great pain, executed naked before all? What human father could so love a group of people who wanted nothing to do with him and were mostly at enmity with him? Probably no man really could. But God the Father did. Not just in His love for lost and fallen humanity, but for His son as well! What, you say? He had His own Son go through that misery out of love for Him? It makes no sense! It certainly makes no sense to our ways of thinking, but God's ways are so vastly differing from man's.

The pain of the crucifixion process was various and intense. It began with Jesus before Caiaphas, the high priest, and the scribes and elders. He was spat on, slapped and beaten (Matthew 26:67). Then the following day when Pilate attempted to let Him be released Jesus suffered the pain of rejection from the very people He had come to save. The people gathered at the trial yelled out with a demonic fervor, *"Let Him be crucified"* (Matthew 27:23). After the trial when the Roman soldiers brought Him into the Praetorian they shoved a crown of thorns on His head which penetrated the scalp. They spat on Him, they beat Him around the head and they mocked Him (Matthew 27:27–30). He then carried the cross in great pain and growing weakness until He no longer had the strength (Matthew 27:32). Finally, naked before the world in great pain, weakness and humility, they drove the spikes through His hands and feet and pierced His side with a spear. Throughout His ordeal – the trial, the mockery, the beatings and the crucifixion, He was silent. As Isaiah had prophesied,

> *"He was oppressed and afflicted, yet he did not open his mouth; he was led like a lamb to the slaughter, and as a sheep before her shearers is silent, so he did not open his mouth."* (Isaiah 53:7 NIV)

Yet, finally Jesus did call out with a great cry. Not so much from the physical pain which must have been horrendous; not from the rejection of man and the betrayal of His disciples; but from a brief separation from the Father as the sin of the world came upon Him as He stood in man's place of judgment.

> *"About the ninth hour Jesus cried out with a loud voice, saying, 'Eli, Eli, lama sabachthani?' that is, 'My God, my God, why have you forsaken me?'"* (Matthew 27:46 NKJV)

In the best of relationships that we know, maybe a great marriage or a lifelong friendship, or a tight-knit family, the depth of love, friendship, intimacy and commitment does not even come close to that which Jesus and the Father had from the beginning of time. Twice that we know of from the gospel accounts the Father spoke of His love and pleasure in Jesus. David, in the spirit, overheard a conversation that had taken place countless millenniums before in Psalm 2. The Father stated to Jesus

"Ask of Me,
and I will surely give the nations as Thine inheritance,
and the very ends of the earth as Thy possession."

(Psalm 2:8 NASB)

And again, David writes,

"The LORD says to my Lord:
'Sit at My right hand,
Till I make Your enemies a footstool.'"

(Psalm 110:1 NKJV)

The Father had from the beginning of time, long before this world was created, intended to give the nations to Jesus. In fact, His deeper purpose in creating mankind was to create a bride for Jesus. And the love, the communion and the fellowship between the Father and the Son was perfect and complete in a way we cannot fully comprehend, because at our best we are not fully capable of selfless love as God is. For all of time that love and intimacy between the Father and Son was complete. But now, as the sin of mankind came on Jesus as our sacrificial lamb, a separation came between the Father and the Son. Because God is absolutely holy, sin cannot be in His immediate glory and presence. Of all the pain Jesus had gone through none of it compared to this. Was ever a such a cry of completely undeserved pain and rejection ever heard before? Likely not, nor will it ever be heard again. We can only guess at what that felt like in Jesus' heart as the Father withdrew His Presence. That pain is what it took to finally raise up a cry from Jesus. And what is so hard to grasp is that the Father willed, ordained and predestined Jesus to go through all of this (Acts 4:27–28).

The overwhelming question is WHY? How could such a loving God not only allow, but ordain such a loved one to go through so much torment? The answer, as difficult as it is, is God's desire that we be a true reflection of Himself. When we say that God is love (1 John 4:8) what are we really saying? Do we even have a model or type of love on earth that can serve as a reflection? Perhaps, to a degree, when we hear of heroic stories. Mothers and fathers sacrificing their lives for sons or daughters. But even in such wonderful displays as those, that love is primarily reserved for immediate family. When Jesus taught on love He said,

> *"If you love those who love you, what credit is that to you? For even sinners love those who love them."*
>
> (Luke 6:32 NASB)

God's definition of love is so broad and generous as to even love His enemies. Jesus was sent to die for us while we were still at enmity with God (1 John 4:10). Jesus stated,

> *"I say to you, love your enemies, and pray for those who persecute you that you may be sons of your Father in heaven."*   (Matthew 5:44–45 NIV)

It must be understood, God's desire is not to merely be nice to us, or even just kind to us as we understand kindness. His intent is to love us to a place of completeness so that we share His holy and compassionate goodness!

His intent in fact, is to love us in such a thorough way as to transform us into a true and living reflection of Himself. The primary means by which He brings us into the lifelong process of conformity to Jesus is the cross! Or to restate it, because God is love He always calls us to make choices out of love. He wants us to choose to be holy just as He, our Father in Heaven is holy.

The problem from our perspective is basically twofold. Firstly, until we really experience a revelation of His glory and holiness we will continue to compare our *relative goodness* in the light of things we have done ourselves in the past, and the things that others are doing, or not doing, in our present. Revelation of God's glory brings about a swift and thorough understanding that the best efforts we can come up with are as filthy rags compared to His holiness. Isaiah the prophet put it this way:

> *"For all of us have become like one who is unclean, and all our righteous deeds are like a filthy garment; and all of us*

wither like a leaf, and our iniquities, like the wind, take us away." (Isaiah 64:6 NASB)

Secondly, we have to come to the point where we realize that apart from His grace and the power of the Holy Spirit, it is impossible to walk in a way pleasing to God. It is only by walking in the Holy Spirit that we can truly experience the fruit of the Spirit – love, joy, peace, self-control, in a growing and constant way (Galatians 5:22–23). Apart from the grace of the ongoing work of the person of God's Spirit within us it is impossible to love God – because God does not measure our love for Him by merely good intentions. He measures our love by obedience! Jesus said,

"If you love me, you will obey what I command." (John 14:15)

At this point, it must be categorically stated that religious legalism does not please God! By legalism I mean reducing our relationship with God to do's and don'ts and thinking God is impressed and pleased with our sacrifices. There are only two things we can really offer up to God that please Him as far as a sacrifice goes; our obedience to Him out of love and a broken and contrite heart.

Obedience born out of love is vastly different from obedience born out of trying to earn something. The former is sonship and the latter is slavery. As Paul stated in Romans 8,

"For you have not received a spirit of slavery leading to fear again, but you have received a spirit of adoption as sons." (Romans 8:15 NASB)

The cross and the cross alone has made us acceptable to the Father. What God is looking for is living, giving and serving out of a loving heart. Serving not out of fear or striving but out of love and gratitude.

Obedience to God out of love produces a consistent, fervent desire to please Him in every action, thought and attitude. It brings us to a posture of growing more and more into a reflection of Jesus, just as His desire was to constantly please the Father. But, the grace to walk in such intimacy and holiness with God only comes by the power of Holy Spirit working in our lives. Our own strength and religious determination is not enough to empower us to walk in holiness. In fact, and here is the heart of the problem, as long as we are trusting in our own strength we are still in a place of pride towards God and others. As if we really could, in ourselves, measure up to His perfect standards. It is the power of brokenness that allows us to really tap into the presence and power of God and it is brokenness that will position us to experience open heavens.

Note

1. *teleioo*, meaning to complete, i.e. (lit.) accomplish, or (fig.) consummate (in character); consecrate, finish, fulfil, (make) perfect.

Chapter 5

The Power of Brokenness (part 2)

True spiritual brokenness is the state of realizing that in and of ourselves we cannot please God. Brokenness is not merely an emotional state or an outward attitude or façade. It is a desperation within our innermost being for more of God. It is an all-consuming desire to both know Him and please Him more fully. And, the good news is, it is brokenness – the continual heartcry for God – which above all else pleases God. David the worshipper stated,

> *"For You do not delight in sacrifice,*
>   *otherwise I would give it;*
> *You are not pleased with burnt offering.*
> *The sacrifices of God are a broken spirit;*
> *a broken and a contrite heart,*
> *O God, Thou wilt not despise."*   (Psalm 51:17 NASB)

In Psalm 42, verse 1, we read,

> *"As the deer pants for streams of water,*
> *so my soul pants for you, O God."*

Brokenness is the quintessential state of being lovesick. It is the realization that one can no longer live without more of God and His grace. It is also the heart faith to realize that God will and must respond to that heartcry because, in His love, He was actually the one who initiated it. David wrote and sang,

*"When You said, 'Seek My face,' my heart said to You,
'Your face, O LORD, I shall seek.'"*   (Psalm 27:8 NASB)

Brokenness is a consuming desperation for more of God's presence and love. It is moving well past the point of satisfaction in past blessings and the promises of what's to come. As one before me has eloquently stated,

> *"It is the realization that our cupboards are barren, our hearts are bankrupt and all we've experienced is worthless in comparison to His great glory".*

Ministering to God or ministering to man?

There is no other book in existence that contains so many poignant stories and situations as the Bible. But probably one of the most moving pictures of demonstrative love in all Scripture however, is that of the woman who cleansed the feet of Jesus with expensive perfume. This must have taken place on at least two different occasions, possibly three. For our purposes we focus on the occasion at the house of Simon the Leper, a religious leader of his day. However, in order to get the full picture we will loosely combine the accounts of Matthew 26, Mark 14, and Luke 7 as well.

According to Luke the woman *"had lived a sinful life in that town"*. Most likely she had been a prostitute who's life had recently been turned around due to Jesus. Jesus was in Simon's house eating and relaxing with His disciples and a number of other guests. The woman, hearing that Jesus was there, entered the house without invitation and began to *"wet his feet with her tears. Then she wiped them with her hair, kissed them and poured perfume on them"* (Luke 7:38). According to three of the gospel accounts she had brought the perfume in an alabaster jar or vial. Alabaster is a fine-grained type of plaster which can be easily broken or cut. By nature it is both somewhat fragile and translucent – much like our hearts! According to the account in Mark, she broke the jar open.

It is critical to realize that this perfume was not ordinary, common-place perfume, but one of extreme value. According to Mark 14:5 it was worth more than a year's wages for an average worker. As she began to pour it out on Jesus, not only the religious scribes and Pharisees who were there, but also some of the disciples began to complain of the waste. After all, the perfume could have been sold for a lot of money and that money given to the poor. Here in a nutshell is the dilemma facing the church today. Which is of greater importance – our ministry to man, or our ministry to God? Again, it is important to realize that some of the critics of this seemingly opulent display were not only the religious leaders, Matthew 26:8 tells us, *"the disciples were indignant when they saw this, and said, 'Why this waste?'"* Often this is the case with ministers of the gospel. We can become so consumed with our vision for ministry to man on behalf of God, that anything – even extravagant worship – that detracts from our ministry to man is considered a waste! To restate the question, which is a higher priority – the the great commission or the great commandment?

In response to the criticisms that this display was wasteful, Jesus gave a rebuke to His disciples. *"Why are you bothering this woman? She has done a beautiful thing to me."* He went on to say that wherever in the world the gospel was preached, her story would be told. Why? Why out of the countless stories that happened during His time on earth would Jesus want this one made into a memorial? Because it demonstrates the very reason Jesus came from heaven to earth – to restore sinners to a place of vital love with God!

Luke's account of the story relates the righteous indignation of the religious leaders towards Jesus for letting this woman, who was publicly regarded as a sinner, touch His feet. Jesus responded to the self-righteous criticisms by saying that when He entered Simon's house no one offered to wash His hands, let alone His feet, which were dirty from walking on dusty streets, probably littered with donkey and camel dung. He said,

> *"I came into your house. You did not give me any water for my feet, but she wet my feet with her tears and wiped them with her hair. You did not give me a kiss, but this woman, from the time I entered, has not stopped kissing my feet. You*

did not put oil on my head, but she has poured perfume on
my feet. Therefore, I tell you, her many sins have been
forgiven – for she loved much. But he who has been forgiven
little loves little." (Luke 7:44–47 NIV)

Simon, and the other religious leaders were mainly concerned with maintaining form, tradition and appearances. The disciples were mainly concerned with ministry to man. The focus of the disciples was certainly better than that of the religious leaders, but both missed the mark. Both fell short of God's highest priority:

"Hear, O Israel: The LORD *is our God, the* LORD *is one. You*
shall love the LORD *your God with all your heart... "*
(Deuteronomy 6:4–5 NASB)

Of course, as Deuteronomy 6:5 continues we discover that we are to love God with our souls (the intellectual knowledge of Him and His ways) and our strength (our service unto Him and others in His Name). But His highest priority is for us to minister to Him! We must ask ourselves the question therefore, "To whom is our best going? To man or to God?"

When this woman poured out her costly perfume, she first did something that is key to understanding God's desire for us. She broke the alabaster jar open (Mark 14:3). She chose to pay the price of transparency with God! This alabaster jar was translucent and fragile. Like alabaster, our hearts are fragile and easily broken – especially in our 21st century culture where commitment in relationships is an increasingly rare commodity. We are so afraid of becoming vulnerable and allowing our hearts to become really desperate for an individual. The traditional wedding vow "for better or worse, 'till death do us part" is, in the vast majority of marriages today is only a quaint, poetic tradition with no real intent behind it. But what God is after is hearts that are broken – opened violently – in desperation for Him. What even the disciples did not realize, yet King David, the lover of God's heart did, was that religious sacrifices in ministry did not impress God. True love is always a choice. The woman who broke open her alabaster vial chose to be broken for God. It is a choice that no one else can vicariously make for you.

In his book *Desire of the Everlasting Hills* Thomas Cahill writes eloquently of the shocking experience the guests at Simon's dinner party must have had when a woman regarded as a prostitute proceeded to wash Jesus' feet with her tears and hair. He writes,

> "The scene is so shocking ... it is difficult to imagine such an excessive woman, cheaply painted, her vulgar apparel chosen for the sake of a teasing display of her physical endowments, bawling her head off and crawling on her knees to the naked feet." [1]

As Cahill correctly points out however, the reason the woman put herself through such a humbling experience in a situation where, surely she knew her presence would be despised, is she knew beyond a shadow of a doubt that Jesus would never reject her, whereas the religious leaders surely would have. This is a woman who exemplifies biblical brokenness. She was living in hopeless lifestyle, used by men, rejected by most women and without any long-term future. From a posture of brokenness she emptied the alabaster jar of her heart and poured it out on the person of Jesus.

It is common when we know someone is very near death to do everything within one's abilities to make that person comfortable. Even condemned murderer's are often given whatever they desire for their last meal. Jesus stated in both Matthew's and Mark's accounts of the story that what the woman in those stories had done by pouring out the perfume from the broken jar was, in effect, to prepare Him for His burial. No doubt in those times, part of the burial preparation was to cover the body in perfume prior to wrapping it for the actual burial. It would have been sign of respect for the deceased, as within a few days the body would begin to stink. But, in Jesus' case the placing of the perfume on Him by this woman before He died was highly significant. Part of it has to do with the commandment for the Levites to have a perfume in the tabernacle which we will examine later on. But, what was significant with Jesus was that the perfume was placed on Him before He dies, not after.

This is entirely hypothetical, but it is just possible that amidst the incredible ordeal of the cross there was just one sweet thing present. It's possible that in the midst of all the pain, suffering, rejection, blood and dirt of the road to Calvary and the ensuing events of the cross, that one sweet smell rose up to Jesus' nostrils – the residue of the costly perfume the woman had used to wash His feet. In the midst of the brutality of man's rejection and the sin of the world separating Him from His Father, possibly that sweet smell reinforced the compelling power of love in His heart that had brought Him to that point.

We know that at the last supper Jesus had washed the disciples feet. He told them *"A person who has had a bath needs only to wash his feet"* (John 13:10). He said to them later in John 15, *"You are already clean because of the word I have spoken to you"* (John 15:3). As the sinless Lamb of God, Jesus had no need to repent, or to be cleansed of any sins. But who would take the place of a lowly servant and wash His feet as He would soon do for His disciples? Apparently no one, except for a woman who was perceived as a sinner by religious people and overly extravagant by the disciples. Except for the central event of the crucifixion this is one of the very few stories found in all four of the gospels. As Jesus said, *"I tell you the truth, wherever the gospel is preached throughout the world, what she has done will also be told, in memory of her."* (Matthew 26:13; Mark 14:9).

This story is not only a memorial to the depths of this woman's fervent love for Jesus, but also a powerful and poignant picture of how precious our love is to God! God is love! Everything He does in our lives is for the reason of love. And with the fragility of relationships today what is so hard to fathom is that our pure devotion to Him, no matter what appearances or traditions dictate, is a fragrant aroma to Him as well. Rather than being ashamed of us, or focusing on our past mistakes and failures, the desire of His heart is for us to unabashedly, and with our whole hearts, love Him and learn to minister to Him. When we break open our hearts and pour them out onto His feet of peace that were bruised for our sakes, our prayers and praise rise up as a sweet aroma to the Lamb of God. It is the one thing we can offer to Him time and time again which is absolutely precious to Him. Not even a lifetime of good works compares with it. That is the fragrant aroma and the soothing oil of a heart that is desperately longing to minister to Him.

A person with a heart of humility – such as Mary sitting at the feet of Jesus, or simply a desperate unknown person of dubious worth in the eyes of the crowd – is the type of person who will find God's presence in increasing measure.

The priceless gift

In the summer of 1998 I received a picture or vision from the Holy Spirit. I saw two friends approach one another. One came with a beautifully gift-wrapped box, about the size of a shoe box. The recipient of the gift could tell the gift must be valuable because of the quality and care of the gift-wrapping – the expensive type that fine stores usually use. He then proceeded to open the gift with great care and anticipation. Inside were a set of cups – beautiful hand-made cups bearing wonderful artwork. It was clear that the cups were of great worth, either because they were hand-made or possibly antique, but there was a problem with them. Each had a crack in them. They were all flawed! The friend who was receiving the gift was a bit puzzled. Why would his good friend give him a set of cracked cups – unless they were purely for decoration? None of the cups could effectively hold any liquids at all. What was the point?

Still, the friend received the gift with thanks, not wanting to be disrespectful of the obvious kind intentions of his friend. However, when he arrived home he did not know what to do with the cups. They could not be used to hold a full cup of coffee – they were of little practical use. He thought of throwing them out, but was sure they must be of some value, being antique. So he took them and put the box on a shelf in the attic.

The picture then changed and I saw someone giving a similar cup to the Lord Jesus. The Lord carefully received the cup in both hands and looked on it with great affection and devotion. He then said to me "Do you know why this cup is so valuable to Me"? "No, I replied". He said "Because, I can fill this vessel with My glory and it will not keep it for itself but will let it flow out to all around it."

When we are self-centered and driven we become like a Cain, or a King Saul – making sacrifices to the Lord, yet always giving Him second best. When we reach the condition of desperate brokenness however, we realize that the best we can possibly do for the Lord is to give ourselves to Him. Of course, we are to give towards the things of God, the works of God, and the people of God, but if we are really going to place the great commandment in its proper priority we must first give of ourselves to Him!

To be broken for the Lord does not mean to continually suffer some kind of hardship. Rather it means we make conscious choices to desire more and more of God and less and less of ourselves. It is to daily echo the prayerful cry of John the Baptist: *"He must increase, but I must decrease"*! To be broken for the Lord is to regularly make the choice "I must have more of God in my life, no matter what the cost". Brokenness is a state of being consumed with the all-consuming fire of God's own Presence. It is a strange sort of homesickness for the throne of heaven, while realizing you've never completely been there to understand what you're homesick for.

Charles G. Finney the great American revivalist of the 19th century wrote an article on things that both hinder and encourage revival. Of the some 22 items he listed which can hinder revival he contended,

"A revival will decline and cease unless Christians are frequently reconverted."

He was not speaking theologically, but was asserting the need for a constant renewal and a fresh hunger for the person of God. He continued to write,

"Christians, in order to keep in the spirit of a revival, commonly need to be frequently convicted and humbled and broken down before God."

This is only really possible by the actual seeking of God Himself. When we move from one realm of glory to another, as Paul wrote, then we experience a deeper and deeper revelation and understanding of the person of God.

Crack addicts say that the first time they do crack the trip is so completely amazing that from then on they will do everything possible, including violent acts, burglary, even prostitute themselves, in order to re-experience that "first time". The problem is, as with all sin, the bondage takes over and the subsequent experiences never quite equal that first time. It becomes a vicious addictive all-consuming hunger which can never be satiated. That first time can never really be duplicated. Revelation of the person of God is just the opposite however. Jesus gives life, and gives it increasingly abundantly. And when we break into even a little bit more of His glory, it is always better than the time before and there will always be much more to come. As the Psalmist wrote,

> *"Great is the* LORD, *and highly to be praised, and His greatness is unsearchable."*   (Psalm 145:3 NASB)

His Glory is unsearchable, or unfathomable as the NIV puts it. No matter how deep we go into the awesome goodness of God's person, we will have always just barely entered in. As St Augustine is credited with saying,

> "God is like a huge circle. No matter how deep into the circle you go you can never come to the center of it."

~~In modern parlance, we could say that God is the best addiction known to man.~~

Jacob, when he wrestled with the angel of the Lord (Genesis 32), refused to let go even when the angel attempted to leave him at daybreak. He held on even to the point of becoming disabled, as the angel dislocated his hip. To be constantly in pursuit of God is disabling to us. We can no longer walk so easily in the ways of the world, yet we can run hard after the person of God. From that time onwards, Jacob no longer walked in the fear of his brother Esau which had dominated his life. He was freer than ever before to walk in the blessing of God. All because Jacob chose to not let go of the Lord! Tommy Tenney in his book *The God Chasers* writes:

> "When 'the fountains of the great deep burst open' in Genesis 7:11 then 'the floodgates of the sky were opened'. When Jesus the fountain of living waters was broken open on Calvary, the floodgates of God's eternal love burst open for mankind. The proof of that was the veil which separated the Holy of Holies from the rest of the temple was torn open as Jesus gave up the Holy Spirit. As it was in the times of Noah, so it was in the times of Jesus. And so it is today. For the church to experience more open heavens we need our hearts to be opened up more for God."

Note

1. Thomas Cahill, *Desire of the Everlasting Hills*, pp. 203–204, Doubleday.

Chapter 6

A Child Shall Lead Them!

During Easter of 1999 I was speaking at a conference in Stavanger, Norway. Several churches gathered for the conference, and as we came together we experienced something very fresh and wonderful in the Holy Spirit. I had ministered in Stavanger a number of times previously. Several of the city's leading pastors had made a strong effort towards unity and building the city church.

The first night of the conference went fairly well. There was good worship, a notable presence of the Lord and a good ministry time. The overall theme of the evening meetings was "Seeking God's Face of Glory" (as opposed to only His hand of blessing). That first night we had ended the ministry time by giving an altar call for those who needed to repent of hidden sins. We made it clear that God is an awesomely holy God, and in order to really "press in" we need to experience His holiness by grace alone! At least a couple of hundred of the 700 people gathered, responded to the appeal and sought to "get right" with the Lord.

The worship on the second night built on the events of the previous evening and it seemed that we were really beginning to press into the throne room. Hebrews 4:16 says, *"Let us then approach the throne of grace with confidence"* – that's exactly what were attempting to do.

We probably worshipped in excess of an hour and I felt it was time to get into the message. I continued with the theme of God's glory, His Presence and seeking His Face. Malachi 3:1 teaches us,

"Behold, I am going to send My messenger, and he will clear the way before Me. And the Lord, whom you seek, will suddenly come to His temple."   (NASB)

This is exactly what took place that evening. Not in totality, of course – that won't begin to happen until the Lord actually returns. But what happened that night was a corporate "breaking through" into a greater presence of God than most there had ever previously experienced. As the meeting continued it was not characterized primarily by outward manifestations of power, or repentance, or anything else. Chiefly the meeting was characterized by God's awesome holiness. Ten or fifteen minutes into the message I found it harder and harder to preach. It wasn't so much that I felt I couldn't speak, rather that it was wrong to continue to speak. All of a sudden, the very Person I was speaking about was there! The Lord whom we were seeking after came suddenly into our midst!

I knew at once that I must not speak any more. The very presence of God – the Holy Spirit – could speak for Himself much more effectively than I could. The sanctuary of the church building could comfortably hold about 600 people. That night there were at least 200 more than that, but despite the overcrowding, you could have heard a pin drop as the glory of the Lord filled the room. I, along with a pastor's wife who was translating for me, simply stood silently on the platform.

I have been in hundreds of meetings in the past where I have received a clear sense of direction from the Holy Spirit as to where we were to go in the meeting. Sometimes into the prophetic, sometimes into repentance, sometimes into different modes of worship, sometimes into praying for people and healings, etc. This, however, was clearly not a time to minister to man. As much as God loves our corporate worship, I knew that the Lord was wanting "more than a song" as Matt Redmond put it.

There are times in worship and prayer where the only thing that really makes sense is to be still before the Lord. It is not so much a posture of listening to the Lord, but rather what could be described as a "gaze of adoration". Psalm 46:10 says,

> "*Be still, and know that I am God;*
> *I will be exalted among the nations,*
> *I will be exalted in the earth."*

Reading the Scriptures and meditating on their truths and principles is of great value; voicing our needs and interceding for others extends the Kingdom of God; but more than anything else we need to simply "gaze" upon the Lord and worship Him unreservedly for who He is.

As the meeting progressed I observed a young man on the front row, worshipping the Lord with joy and celebrating, with tears streaming down his cheeks. There was a radiance about him. His face was almost shining. This young man was having far more than a mere emotional experience. As I looked on him a particular scripture came to mind. A scripture that speaks prophetically of the immense impact that the Lord Jesus will have upon the earth as it becomes "full of the knowledge of the Lord."

> "*A shoot will come up from the stump of Jesse; from his roots a Branch will bear fruit. The Spirit of the* Lord *will rest on him – the Spirit of wisdom and of understanding, the Spirit of counsel and of power, the Spirit of knowledge and of the fear of the* Lord *– and he will delight in the fear of the* Lord*. He will not judge by what he sees with his eyes, or decide by what he hears with his ears; but with righteousness he will judge the needy, with justice he will give decisions for the poor of the earth. He will strike the earth with the rod of his mouth; with the breath of his lips he will slay the wicked. Righteousness will be his belt and faithfulness the sash around his waist. The wolf will live with the lamb, the leopard will lie down with the goat, the calf and the lion and the yearling together; and a little child will lead them. The cow will feed with the bear, their young will lie down together, and the lion will eat straw like the ox. The infant will play near the hole of the cobra, and the young child put his hand into the viper's nest. They will neither harm nor*

destroy on all my holy mountain, for the earth will be full of
the knowledge of the LORD as the waters cover the sea."
                                        (Isaiah 11:1–9 NIV)

This powerful passage prophesies many things – most likely different events that will occur at different times in the future. It speaks of the coming of Jesus, the Messiah, the Son who came to make peace. But it also points of a time when the purposes of Jesus on earth are much more greatly fulfilled than today. It is also a passage that I consider of great importance for me personally. Along with Habakkuk, 2:14 which echoes it saying,

> *"For the earth will be filled with the knowledge of the glory of*
> *the LORD, as the waters cover the sea."*

So many years previously when I saw the vision of a huge and majestic Jesus over the hills of San Diego, I knew that in my lifetime the outpouring of God's Spirit throughout the world was going to increase exponentially.

Becoming "childlike" in our ways

A key element of the passage in Isaiah 11 is the picture that people are being led into righteousness and abundant life by a "child". In the one sense, we understand this as a picture of Jesus, who as the only begotten Son of God, lived to please His Heavenly Father. Jesus was, and is, the perfect "child of God". Not *childish*, but *childlike* in the quality of His relationship with His Father.

Having a childlike relationship with the Father is another key element that we must possess, both individually and corporately, in order to position ourselves to experience God's open heavens. The Bible expresses this wisdom of God and illustrates it in a variety of ways. According to both Luke 18:17 and Mark 10:15 Jesus asserted,

> *"Truly I say to you, whoever does not receive the kingdom of*
> *God like a child will not enter it at all."*   (NASB)

This statement is important in helping us to understand that the Father desires His children to look to Him and respond to Him *as children*. But, it is also critical in helping us to understand the attitude of the heart we are to have towards God. In Evangelical Protestant Christianity there has been a major focus on systematic theology now for several generations of the church. Whilst providing us with a rich heritage of theological understanding, such an approach can lead to an unspoken danger in the church as believers relate almost exclusively to God through their intellects. The result can be a loss of a "sense of awe" towards God. When a Christian, especially a church leader, leans exclusively on his, or her, *head knowledge*, rather than *heart knowledge* of God, the result will invariably be a pharisaical spirit.

That is not to deny the value of a balanced and thorough understanding of the Scriptures. But, the "pharisee" will always reject anything from God that cannot be understood and dissected by rational analysis. The pharisee will also tend to reject anything that does not fit with their previous experience. Not only does that leave very little room for the prophetic and the leading of the Holy Spirit, but I believe, leaves little but dry and boring religious rituals for the church to follow. In such a scenario, worship becomes a mere preparation for the preaching. At worst, worship and prayer can be perceived as exercises, traditions or rituals to be performed. The Irish singer and song writer Van Morrison, in a song written some ten years ago about the Lord Jesus Christ, wrote, "Didn't I come to give you a sense of wonder, didn't I come to give you a sense of awe." Childlikeness has at its center an awesome respect of the Father.

The Bible says that in the early days of the Church, *"Everyone was filled with awe"* (Acts 2:43). The people lived a lifestyle of fellowship, ministry, community, worship and prayer, and were continually experiencing God's grace in such a remarkable way that there was no room for complacency or boredom. This is a far cry from much of the church in the western world today, where many Christians even struggle to attend church each Sunday morning to worship the Lord for just a short time.

One of the favorite things that I did with my children, especially when they were younger, was watching the Disney animated classics together – movies like *Dumbo* or *Pinocchio*. Part of the fun of watching the movie was simply observing how spellbound my kids were as they saw life situations, stretched by imagination and animation, beyond what reality could possibly offer. As kids, they just appreciated what they saw – never questioning the validity of what was taking place. As adults, we watch with a supposedly discerning eye – knowing that such situations and characters are merely make-believe. Yet, we often transfer our cerebral assessment of situations and experiences to our faith. But, our God is not bound by any limitations. He is not confined to working within the parameters of our finite imaginations. He is the God of the past, the present, and the future. He is the all-powerful One who spoke and the earth, moon, stars and oceans came into being.

With such an awesome God to worship and love, why is it that most often our times of worship are restricted by the limitations of our church programs and schedules, rather than being characterized by a childlike sense of wonder and appreciation? The young man I was watching that night in Stavanger was gloriously lost in his childlike adoration and wonder of the goodness of God. We should aim to be the same!

In Matthew chapter 18 Jesus was asked by His disciples who was greatest in the Kingdom of God. To make a graphic illustration to them, He called a nearby child to Himself and then stated,

> *"Whoever then humbles himself as this child, he is the greatest in the kingdom of heaven."* (Matthew 18:4 NASB)

Jesus knew that the most effective of God's children would be those who were willing to trust Him unquestioningly and to obey Him with an open, childlike faith and acceptance of His will.

The beauty of most children is their inherent ability to give themselves over wholeheartedly and with a singularity of purpose, to whatever they are doing at the moment.

Whether it's watching an animated cartoon, playing with building blocks or enjoying an ice-cream cone, they focus on the task at hand and manage to block out all other distractions. We adults however, are rarely fully employed, body, soul and spirit, with what we have at hand. I suspect this is why the last few years have seen an increase in activities that it labels "extreme"; extreme sports, extreme sex, etc. Humanity is desperate for something to give itself to that can be fully captivating!

Losing our dignity

God created us with a void which only He can fill, and He knows that we can only be truly fulfilled when He becomes the undistracted center of our attention and desires in this childlike way. The Bible says that God desires us to love Him with all of our heart, soul and strength. David's heart reflected this childlike exuberance in love and worship for God. We read of him leaping and dancing before the Lord with all of his strength when bringing the Ark of God's glory into the city (2 Samuel 6:14). He was beside himself with joy that the actual glory of God, as known by Moses, was coming into the city. His wife Michael however, despised his enthusiasm for God. Both 2 Samuel 14:16 and 1 Chronicles 15:29 say that she "despised him in her heart". Her adult sense of dignity and decorum was offended by David's childlike, single-minded enthusiasm for God.

When David returned to the palace after placing the Ark in the tent prepared for it, Michael rebuked David for his public display.

> *"How the king of Israel distinguished himself today! He uncovered himself today in the eyes of his servants' maids as one of the foolish ones shamelessly uncovers himself."*
> (2 Samuel 6:20 NASB)

David had taken off his royal robe and worn a priest's ephod in order to worship the Lord. Michael was offended that he had stooped from his place of stature and authority in order to take on the appearance of a "commoner". However, David responded to her,

> *"I will celebrate before the* L<small>ORD</small>. *I will become even more undignified than this, and I will be humiliated in my own eyes."* (2 Samuel 6:21–22 NASB)

It would be religious rather than spiritual to make a ritual or program out of dancing or any other outward expression. David danced because the joy of the Lord was bubbling up from within him. The Holy Spirit prompted him to do it. Michael had a stoic, austere response to the person of God. The price she paid according to verse 23 was barrenness all the days of her life. The price she paid for her adult, sophisticated approach to God was a terrible one. Certain behavior and expressions in worship, prayer and ministering to God, should never be made into a ritual. But equally the lack of any outward expression can in itself become a ritual and a way of life.

Have you ever marveled that on even the hottest and most humid days children will still go outside and run themselves ragged until they're hot, tired and sweaty? Such behavior on days like that make most adults shake their heads, but the children are doing what comes naturally to them – playing wholeheartedly. When we read in the Psalms about worship, we read of standing, lifting hands, yelling, dancing, playing with loud instruments. When we read in the Bible about prayer, we read of weeping before the Lord, calling out to God. When we read about Jesus we read of Him praying fervently – so much so, that in the garden before His crucifixion He even sweated blood.

We read of Jesus that,

> *"During the days of Jesus' life on earth, he offered up prayers and petitions with loud cries and tears to the one who could save him from death."* (Hebrews 5:7 NIV)

His praying was enthusiastic to say the least! Often, when we think of a couple in love, a romantic picture comes to mind of the two sharing a picnic on a green meadow complete with spring flowers; or perhaps of a candlelit dinner under the stars at an outdoor café in the summer. Those romantic scenes are, for sure, a valid and enjoyable part of the relationship – but that's not what produces babies! It is the fervent and completely engaging behavior of two adults who are lost in a moment of passion for one another that produces babies! Too often, we in the contemporary western church resemble David's wife Michael – dignified but barren, rather than fervent and passionate, filled with God's grace like David!

At the meetings in Stavanger I came to realize that most of us who were in adulthood needed a "grace" from God to enable us to come back to the childlike freedom of losing our self-consciousness in our adoration of Him. We need the ability to lose ourselves in worship to God just as David did before the ark.

As I observed the young man at those meetings who was worshipping God so enthusiastically, I suggested that anyone who wanted an "impartation" to enable them to give themselves more freely to God, should come forward and be prayed for by him and the pastors. For the next couple of hours some 700 people quietly queued around the room and passed before the prayer team. For the most part I just stood back to try to take in what was happening. It was unlike any other meeting I had ever been in. During that period no one was really speaking and very few left. People just quietly, slowly and in an attitude of worship, walked through the line. You could sense the shekinah glory of God – the weight of His Presence was hanging over the room.

I was transfixed, watching people as they passed though the prayer line. There were a few people collapsing from the power of the Lord, but for the most part I could almost visibly see a transition taking place in people's hearts as they passed through. Because the line was moving slowly as the group of some ten people prayed for each person, I could easily track people. As they drew near to be prayed for, their attention moved from giving worship to the Lord, to receiving love from Him.

As people approached you could see a range of emotions evident on their faces. Some looked peaceful, some joyful, while others showed tell-tale signs of deep frustration, loneliness and failure, but almost everyone who passed through the line came out visibly different. You could almost see lines of worry or fear, replaced with a deep peace. You could see hopelessness replaced by hope, faith and love. For many it was like the experience of a child who had been inadvertently separated from his/her parents and suddenly returned to their safety and comfort. Through countless church meetings spanning almost 25 years, I don't think I can remember a meeting where so many people have been so deeply impacted in a corporate sense!

Intimacy versus religion

We live in a time of ever increasing stress. Even as this book was being finalized, the world was still reeling from the September 11th bombing of the twin towers in New York City. The repercussions of that act of terrorism has affected people's peace of mind, as well as the world economy in historic proportions. We are indeed in the time Jesus spoke of in Matthew 24 – a time of wars, and rumors of wars, earthquakes, famines and droughts. Jesus said that the last days would be a time of wars, and rumors of wars. From the time we enter into early adulthood, until we leave this realm, we are constantly surrounded by the pressures of choice and responsibility. The consequences of wrong decisions can drastically effect our health, relationships and finances. Increasingly we see people turning from everything from Prosac to pieces of crystal in an attempt to find some sort of peace. We long for the simplicity of those days when the most serious question we faced was "Who are we going to play with today" and "Do we get dessert tonight?" In the midst of trying to enjoy adulthood with all it has to offer, there is still a childlike cry within us prompted by the Holy Spirit that only God the Father can fill (Romans 8:15).

Jesus said,

> *"I am the way and the truth and the life."*   (John 14:6)

Jesus, through His death and resurrection, removed that which separated us from God the Father – our sins. Because that veil has been torn, intimacy, rather than mere religion is again a real possibility!

In his letter to the church of Rome Paul affirms the possibility of freedom through Christ, and of our childlike states:

> *"For you did not receive a spirit that makes you a slave again to fear, but you received the Spirit of sonship. And by him we cry, 'Abba, Father'."*   (Romans 8:15 NIV)

God's Holy Spirit within each Christian is constantly prompting a cry within our hearts. On a spiritual level that cry is the equivalent of a young child crying out for an embrace from a mother or father. In one of David's Psalms he sang,

> *"How priceless is your unfailing love!*
> *Both high and low among men*
> *find refuge in the shadow of your wings.*
> *They feast on the abundance of your house;*
> *you give them drink from your river of delights."*
>   (Psalm 36:7–8 NIV)

The picture is of people from all walks of life, seeking refuge under the wings of God our protector and provider.

There is, to be sure, a very real comfort and strength that can be drawn from the promises and precepts of God. There is, however also a very real living peace, joy, and comfort that only flows from the very person of God as we draw near to His Person. And the closer we get to God the more transforming His Presence becomes. The apostle Paul confirms this vital process:

> *"Therefore, since we have such a hope, we are very bold. We are not like Moses, who would put a veil over his face to keep the Israelites from gazing at it while the radiance was fading away. But their minds were made dull, for to this day the same veil remains when the old covenant is read. It has not been removed, because only in Christ is it taken away. Even to this day when Moses is read, a veil covers their hearts. But*

whenever anyone turns to the Lord, the veil is taken away.
Now the Lord is the Spirit, and where the Spirit of the Lord is,
there is freedom. And we, who with unveiled faces all reflect
the Lord's glory, are being transformed into his likeness with
ever-increasing glory, which comes from the Lord, who is the
Spirit."   (2 Corinthians 3:12–18 NIV)

The Bible tells us that Moses was the only man that God
spoke to, mouth to mouth, in this earthly realm (Numbers
12:6–8). But what the Bible and church history also teach us
is that we can seek the face of God. In fact it is His fervent
desire that corporately as the people of God we do so
(2 Chronicles 7:14). Although we might not have the same
depth of experience as Moses had, we can by God's grace,
know Him! In fact, according to Paul the glory Moses
experienced would fade after a while – hence his veil. But,
we who have received the cleansing power of the blood
of the Lamb can choose to freely go from glory to ever-
increasing glory. And that glory as Paul wrote, is a transforming glory.

A good pastor or elder will, in the course of his or her
ministry, serve the church by preaching, teaching, counsel-
ing, exhorting and praying. As we sow into the Body of
Christ the word and encouragement of God, we tend to see
increasing maturity and fruitfulness. But when a revelation
of God's glory and goodness comes, it transforms the hearts
and souls of the people. That is to say, that which often takes
countless sermons to achieve, can be accomplished by the
presence of God in seconds! Experiencing the glory of God,
as opposed to merely hearing *about* God, is the difference
between a blind man seeing colors for the first time or merely
hearing about what they look like from another.

Countless men and women throughout the Bible and
church history have had their entire lives turned around by
just a brief revelation of God's glory. The sinner goes from
boasting of his sinful habits to a living hatred of sin and a
consuming desire to please God. The lukewarm Christian
goes from fighting the desire to stay away from church to
longing to be in worship services. The apostles in the upper
room went from being a group of frightened, unsure men

and women to being catalysts for the explosive success of the early Church – all because of a brief release of the fire of God's Presence!

As Jesus said,

> *"I tell you the truth, anyone who will not receive the kingdom of God like a little child will never enter it."*
>
> (Luke 18:17 NIV)

We need to allow God's passion for us to transform our hearts and fill us with a new passion for Him. In the midst of all of the trials, tribulations, and the diversions of life, we must recapture the singular focus of the wonder of God and His Presence. We've been trying to operate as adults out of a mastery of theology, tradition and methodology. Now we must relearn how to delight our hearts in God from a sense of wonder, rather than a utilitarian "what's in it for me?" perspective.

Paul wrote of a grave concern he had for the church in Corinth:

> *"I am afraid that just as Eve was deceived by the serpent's cunning, your minds may somehow be led astray from your sincere and pure devotion to Christ."*
>
> (2 Corinthians 11:3 NIV)

What beguiled Eve was a lie from the enemy that if only Man could gain enough knowledge they could be "as God" – that they could take control of their lives and destinies. Rather, let us allow the cry of the Holy Spirit within us – "Abba Father" – to rise up afresh. We've seen what the church can do when we're in charge. What could happen if we assume the child-like attitude of Jesus' heart and only do what "we see the Father doing"? We could possibly experience the fulfillment of God's sacred promises for our generations.

Chapter 7

Where Are the Levites? (part 1)

I can't remember exactly the first time it happened, but beginning in the mid to late 1990s, I began on occasion to smell sweet smells in certain church meetings and conferences. I had seen countless manifestations over the years from a variety of sources. Some were caused by the power, joy, or new wine of the Holy Spirit coming upon people. Some were due to demonic manifestations in meetings where, as Jesus said in Matthew 12:28, demons were driven out by the kingdom of God coming near. Also there were people who responded to the messages and the ministry in a "soulish" way out of learned behavior or the need for attention. But this manifestation was something completely new and completely beyond the power of anyone to make it happen, short of bringing in lots of fresh flowers or burning incense! In fact, good friends of mine had recently been in meetings where there was such a strong smell of smoke during intense times of worship, that some of the church workers actually began to search for a fire!

Although it was irregular, and definitely not sought for, these tokens of the presence of God began to take place. Sometimes there would be a strong smell of flowers, such as from a bouquet of roses, or sometimes a sweet scent, such as perfume or incense, would begin to waft through the room. And although neither I nor other ministers present had ever prayed for such manifestations (except symbolically – welcoming the sweet presence of the Holy Spirit etc.), I began to notice a common thread to those kinds of meetings.

It would usually begin to be noticed after there had either been prolonged worship and/or a message concerning either the sweetness of the Lord and/or the consuming fire of His presence.

Please do not misunderstand me here. I never look for manifestations to validate a meeting. In fact, I never pray for them to take place at all – except that is for healings and miracles. But when legitimate manifestations do take place as a result of God's nearness – such as healings, miracles, joy and uncontrollable laughter from the Holy Spirit, weeping, etc., we need to realize that, in part anyway, they are a sign and wonder. Something supernatural and extraordinary is taking place and it could be God is releasing it at that time and place in order to get our attention.

Chasing hard after God

There are those who, unfortunately, seek after manifestations more than they seek God. There are almost always extremists in any area of life. However, there are too many pharisees who automatically dismiss the genuine experiences others have had with God as mere emotionalism. To those critics who would say of Charismatics and Pentecostals that they are just after an experience, I would respond that the people of the Bible who dramatically impacted their times and cultures for God often began their ministries with life-changing supernatural experiences of God. In fact, they often had the type of encounters with God that present-day pharisees say no longer happen. Possibly that is why the contemporary church in the western nations has seemingly had so little impact on the world around us! We have, by and large, not been encouraged to radically seek the face of God.

There is beginning to rise up however, a people who are taking as a motto David's heartcry, as found in Psalm 63:8:

> *"My soul followeth hard after thee."*   (KJV)

These type of people can be chiefly characterized as people who love God, believe in the gospel and are attempting to live biblically-based lives, but are still not satisfied. They are desperate for more of God Himself. Their lives are not driven by the desire for more money, or blessings concerning material things. And they are not confusing their ministry to man with their ministry to the person of God. They are after far more than a mere manifestation – they simply cannot live without more of Him!

If their attraction was to another human being we would label them "love sick", and we usually find that acceptable. In fact, many of us have spent countless hours reading books and watching movies about men and women who because of being "love sick" heroically overcame incredible obstacles in the pursuit of their lover.

Tommy Tenney calls such people "God chasers" in his book by the same name. *God chaser* is a term David would identify with if he were here today. A.W. Tozer, perhaps the greatest Bible teacher to emerge out of North America in the last 100 years had this to say in the preface of his book *The Pursuit of God*:

> "Within the fold of conservative Christianity there are to be found increasing numbers of persons whose religious lives are marked by a growing hunger after God Himself. They are eager for spiritual realities and will not be put off with words, nor will they be content with correct 'interpretations' of truth. They thirst for God, and they will not be satisfied till they have drunk deep at the Fountain of Living Water."

In biblical terms I would refer to these people as "The Levites of the Body of Christ".

We know that there were twelve tribes of the Israelite people, including what is now referred to as "the lost tribe". All of the twelve tribes had different characteristics and a uniqueness, just as any twelve families gathered together would. When we read Jacob's blessings over his twelve sons in Genesis 49:1–28, we gain some insight into the difference between them. The twelve sons, were in turn the fathers of the twelve tribes who subsequently took on their personalities, complete with their corresponding strengths and weaknesses. We see these families, or tribal traits, reflected again over 400 years later when Moses gives blessings to the twelve tribes shortly before he dies (Deuteronomy chapter 33).

Perhaps the most informative passage concerning the Levites however, can be found in the Book of Joshua chapter 13. This is Joshua's version of Moses' final blessing to the Israelites near the end of his own days. In this chapter he gives recognition to the distribution of the lands they have captured to each of the tribes, just as Moses had promised them years before. Each tribe received a portion of land to settle in. Some of the tribes were given great cities that the Hebrews had captured from their enemies; some tribes were given beautiful wooded areas and others fertile farmlands; some were given mountainous areas and some had great rivers and lakes. But there was one tribe that actually received no land for their inheritance whatsoever – the Levites. In truth though, they received the greatest inheritance of all.

> *"But to the tribe of Levi he gave no inheritance, since the offerings made by fire to the* Lord, *the God of Israel, are their inheritance, as he promised them."*   (Joshua 13:14)

Truly, truly

According to the New American Standard translation of the Bible there are some 25 statements in the Gospels made by Jesus in which He begins by saying *"Truly, truly"*. The King James version reads *"Verily, verily"*, and the New International Version renders the same phrase *"I tell you the truth"*. Although I am no expert in Bible languages, I very much prefer the way the NAS phrases it. "Truly, truly" grabs your attention and you know that Jesus is about to say something that He really wants people to catch. Every word that proceeds from the mouth of God is wisdom and life for those who live by them, but there are certain passages that are absolutely vital, which is why Jesus clearly emphasized their importance by beginning them, *"Truly, truly"*. I bring these passages to mind because we see something similar regarding the inheritance of the Levites.

Although there are no "Truly, truly" verses in the Old Testament, there are in a few places which are equivalent. In certain texts it's as if the Holy Spirit is saying to us "Pay attention. Here is something of critical importance and you really need to get this." The way that He does that is to state the same verse twice essentially. One such passage is found in Joshua 13 when Joshua blesses the tribes with their inheritance, and it occurs with the affirmation of the Levite's inheritance in particular. Again we read in Joshua 13:14:

> *"But to the tribe of Levi he gave no inheritance, since the offerings made by fire to the Lord, the God of Israel, are their inheritance, as he promised them."*   (NIV)

Joshua then continues for the next eighteen verses speaking about some of the other tribes' inheritances and then comes back to the Levites. In fact the inheritance, or seemingly the lack thereof, is the only one mentioned by Joshua twice. He reiterates in verse 32,

> *"But to the tribe of Levi, Moses had given no inheritance; the Lord, the God of Israel, is their inheritance, as he promised them."*

Possibly, if you were a member of the tribe of the Levites present on that day, you would have had a major disappointment. After all, where are your *"large, flourishing cities you did not build, houses filled with all kinds of good things you did not provide, wells you did not dig, and vineyards and olive groves you did not plant"*? The very things that Moses had promised the people that God would give them in the land flowing with *"milk and honey"* (Deuteronomy 6:11), they were seemingly not to going to get! Certainly to many today who measure prosperity by the same standards as the world, it would have seemed rather dismal compared to the other tribes. The truth however, is that the Levites received the greatest of all inheritances. They received the one thing that no amount of silver or gold, good works, or personal sacrifice could ever buy. They received an invitation to come close to the very person of God Himself in the Holy of Holies. And of all the twelve tribes they were the only ones allowed to do so!

Today, in New Covenant times we understand, as Jeremiah put it, that:

> *" 'They will all know me, from the least of them to the greatest,' declares the* LORD.*"*   (Jeremiah 31:34 NIV)

Because of the payment of our sins at the cross by Jesus we can all come to know God by surrendering our lives to Him. And when we do so God places His "Spirit of Adoption" within our hearts and we become born again into the family of God. The question then is, where do we go from there? What do we live for?

Servants or sons?

There are those groups and churches within Christendom that mainly see the Bible from a posture of legalism – as a good instruction manual of do's and don'ts. In such a mind-set God is perceived as more of a judge than a loving Father. For them the blessings of the Kingdom of God only come if they manage to live successfully by all the rules and finally "make it" to Heaven. Then there are those who are captured by God's love for the lost and hurting. For them the Kingdom of God is more about the job at hand now, than the "sweet by-and-by" to come. There is some validity in both views. Of course the Bible is an instruction manual for life. And it goes without saying that the Bible clearly expresses God's heart for the hurt, the broken, and the lost. But above all the Bible, the *Logos*, reveals God the Father's great love for each of us and His desire that we learn to respond to Him in love. In fact God embodies love. He is love! (1 John 4:8, 16). He is the first, the last, and the final definition of love. And because He is love He calls us to be lovers. In fact He calls us to have a joyous abandonment for Him that reflects the feelings that He has for us.

Many would say, "We'll, I'll show you my love for God – just look at all my good works and the sacrifices I make for God." But if one truly loves God, then that individual is also going to love the people God loves. If our hearts are truly captured by God's heart, then we are also captivated by His love for others. It can't be one or the other, it has to be both/and. And true love for the lost, the hurting, the prisoners, and the widows and orphans, compels us to good works. There is a great danger in measuring our love for God by our ministry to man and our personal sacrifice though. It is possible for that ministry to become an idol in itself. In this world it is possible to find many people *serving God*, but who have no time for Him personally. It is this trap that Jesus warned about in Matthew's Gospel.

> *"Not everyone who says to me, 'Lord, Lord,' will enter the kingdom of heaven, but only he who does the will of my Father who is in heaven. Many will say to me on that day, 'Lord, Lord, did we not prophesy in your name, and in your name drive out demons and perform many miracles?' Then I will tell them plainly, 'I never knew you. Away from me, you evildoers!'"* (Matthew 7:21–23 NIV)

It is an easy and dangerous mistake for the Christian servant, whether paid or volunteer, to focus the eyes of their heart more on themselves serving God, than the actual person of God. That image of ourselves as a "good servant" can, just as much as the idolatry of anything else, begin to control our hearts and egos. Such idolatry is in evidence today among leaders whose hearts and messages are focused more on their own ministry, calling and vision, than on simply loving, worshipping and obeying God. And if anyone becomes a perceived threat to their idol, they retaliate in much the same way as Nebuchadnezzar did when Shadrach, Meshach and Abednego refused to bow down to his idol. In the fury of his ego he ordered the furnace to be heated seven times hotter than usual and had them thrown in. One of the easiest ways to know when a supposed servant of God is in such bondage is the continual fire of anger surrounding them due to their raging ego.

Another potential trap is to confuse the anointing of God for the person of God. It is possible, as Balaam found out, to move in the anointing of God, but not be the *friend* of God. It is one thing to seek after God for the power of the Holy Spirit, but another thing altogether to simply want to experience the power of the Holy Spirit through a pure desire to spend time with God. It can be one thing to move in the power and revelation of the Holy Spirit, and another to have a lifestyle of worship in your heart. It's not for nothing that Paul interrupted his treatise on the spiritual gifts in 1 Corinthians chapters 12 and 14 by a statement affirming the pre-eminence of love in the use of the gifts in chapter 13.

> *"If I speak in the tongues of men and of angels, but have not love, I am only a resounding gong or a clanging cymbal. If I have the gift of prophecy and can fathom all mysteries and all knowledge, and if I have a faith that can move mountains, but have not love, I am nothing. If I give all I possess to the poor and surrender my body to the flames, but have not love, I gain nothing."*
> (1 Corinthians 13:1–3 NIV)

It's one thing to be the servant of God, but another to be the friend of God. God has many servants in the church, but unfortunately He has few friends that just want to seek Him for the sake of spending time with Him.

So what is the great call on us, if not to serve one another? What is the gospel all about? The answer is best understood in the powerful simplicity of Jesus' words. In John 14:6 Jesus spoke one of the most profound and significant verses in the entire New Testament – *"I am the way and the truth and the life"* – but He did not stop there. He continued by saying, *"No one comes to the Father except through me."* Jesus came to earth and became the sacrificial Lamb of God, not just to provide us with free life insurance, but to restore us to a living relationship with God the Father, and Himself (John 17:3). Some of the apostles in their writing referred to the Father as *"The Father of glory – the God of our Lord Jesus Christ"* (Ephesians 1:17). He is the One whom Daniel calls the *"Ancient of Days"* (Daniel 7:9, 13, 22).

How radical was, and is, the Father's love for us? Zealous enough for Him to send His only begotten Son to die one of the most painful, shameful and humiliating deaths known to man. John 3:16 reads,

> *"For God so loved the world, that He gave His only begotten Son."*

This is love – the free gift of something most precious to your heart in order to gain someone else's heart. It was because of the Father's passion for us that Jesus came and did what He did.

Losing our lives to gain them

What many in the Body of Christ are waking up to today, is that in many ways we have substituted an intellectual knowledge of God for a passion for Him. We often confuse insights for transformation. We sometimes confuse critical perspectives of doctrine with the cost of discipleship. It's time we took a fresh look at the primary things the Father is after from His sons and daughters. And, possibly, that begins with a fresh perspective on worship and prayer – the two gates of intimacy God has given us.

There can be no true substitute for the greatest commandment which is to *"Love the Lord, our God with all our heart, mind, and strength"*. Not good works, not the studying of endless books, nor the practice of religious tradition. The Father, the Ancient of Days, the God and Father of our Lord Jesus Christ, is searching for true worshippers. God is after people who are as passionate about Him as He is about us. He is looking for a people who will love Him with an abandonment for Him which somehow reflects His great love for us.

In the Chapter 1 we discussed the forerunner spirit of John the Baptist. And it is true that prior to every strong move of the Spirit of God there are prophetic people who help to prepare the way. But, the hearts of those forerunners are primarily motivated by a love for God rather than ministry to man. We see that heart exemplified in John the Baptist, who rather than clinging to his ministry before the crowds proclaimed *"He must increase, but I must decrease"*. John's life from the time he leapt in the womb as a baby when his mother encountered the pregnant mother of Jesus, to leaving his family and living in the desert, to the time of losing his head, was one of running hard after God. His love and pursuit of God was greater than his passion for life. We need to remember, that although John never ministered in a temple or synagogue, he was a Levite – the son of Zacharias – a priest. He was one consumed with desire to draw near to God, and in doing so prepared the way for the true Christ. He referred to himself as a *"friend of the Bridegroom"* (John 3:29).

The path into, not only the things of God, but the very presence of God, always involves the cross. There are no shortcuts that tradition, methodology or education can provide for us. There is only one thing God is really after. Not even our religious sacrifices will suffice. God is after broken hearts. He is after a people willing to pick up their crosses in their love for Him and pursue Him. And without embracing the cross there will never be any resurrection power!

Jesus said,

> *"Whoever tries to keep his life will lose it, and whoever loses his life will preserve it."*   (Luke 17:33 NIV)

This truth is nowhere more evident than when seeking God's Face. It does cost to come close to His presence. He is a consuming fire and there is a burning of the soul one must encounter if one is really going to gaze upon God. We in the western Church have often a perception problem when it comes to viewing God in these terms however. We sometimes have a view of God that lies somewhere between Santa Claus and the state lottery. We want God to give us what we want, when we want it and how we want. Make no mistake, God does intend to give us the desires of our hearts. But with that truth, the rest of the package must be unwrapped. Firstly, our hearts are deceptively evil, as Jeremiah stated. Some of the time the longings of our hearts first need to be sifted by the Holiness of God, or the thing we think we want the most may prove to be our downfall. Secondly, when we pray and sing in our Sunday morning services "All I want is You, Lord" we are often doing so with very little revelation of the awesome Holiness of God. It's not that God doesn't love us just as we are – He does! But, He loves us too much to leave us right where we are.

How to enter the Holy of Holies

So we find ourselves asking the Lord to *"take us past the brazen altars of the outer court and bring us into the Holy of Holies"*. Do we really understand what we are asking for? Probably not, but still that is the prayer the Holy Spirit is raising up within us as He cries out *"Abba, Father"* in the language of our hearts.

In the tabernacles of Moses and Solomon there were three different and distinct courts, or areas to enter. Each represented a more intimate level of relating to God. First there was the outer court, then the Holy Place, and finally the Holy of Holies. The Outer Court was where the Burnt Offering Altar and Laver could be found. The Holy Place and the Holy of Holies comprised the Tabernacle Sanctuary which was center and towards the west end of the Outer Court. The Tabernacle Sanctuary was a wooden structure overlaid with gold. Nothing of the gold or details of the sanctuary were visible in the outer court because of the four coverings over the sanctuary.

In Psalm 100 the psalmist wrote a song of powerful worship to God. It is truly a song which evokes both a passion and an energy in the coming before Him. It reads,

> *"Shout for joy to the LORD, all the earth.*
> *Worship the LORD with gladness;*
> * come before him with joyful songs.*
> *Know that the LORD is God.*
> * It is he who made us, and we are his;*
> * we are his people, the sheep of his pasture.*
> *Enter his gates with thanksgiving*
> * and his courts with praise;*
> * give thanks to him and praise his name."*
>
> (Psalm 100:1–4 NIV)

These verses not only give us strong encouragement to worship God, they also give us great insight in how to come into the gates of the temple and the courts of the Tabernacle. First with thanksgiving – the expression of thanks for His daily mercies and care. Thanksgiving for all He has done and the promise of what is to come. But, if we are to press further in something more is required – worship, or adoration of who He is. Now we are going beyond mere "singing"; we are beginning to minister to Him as opposed to just singing *about* Him. We are beginning to thank Him for who He is, as opposed to what we've received from Him. This is the ticket, or pass, which enables us to enter the Outer Court. And, we find in the Outer Court provision for both cleansing and offering acceptable sacrifices to God so that we might proceed even closer!

The Holy Place, and especially the Holy of Holies, required much more than thanksgiving. The Holy of Holies demanded sacrifice. When we think of our sacrifices to God, we think perhaps of the time, energy and money we've put into the church, or possibly of the effort we've put into reaching out to our neighbors, or ministering to the poor. Perhaps a missions trip we did earlier in the year comes to mind. But, as much as all of these can be genuine expressions of our love for God, His world, and the Church, they are not the sacrifices which qualify us to really enter into the glory of His Presence. That sacrifice is much more costly! It requires the sacrifice of a broken and contrite heart!

> *"For You do not delight in sacrifice,*
> *otherwise I would give it;*
> *You are not pleased with burnt offering.*
> *The sacrifices of God are a broken spirit;*
> *A broken and a contrite heart,*
> *O God, You will not despise."*   (Psalm 51:16–17 NASB)

In short, God is after a people who are as desperate for Him as He was for us. Desperate enough to know that His love is calling us to an all-consuming love. A love where no amount of blessings, or things, can even come close to the need for Him. King David realized this and in his words in Psalm 51 we see the revelation of the sacrifice that God finds truly acceptable – a heart that is burning for His burning, consuming presence.

What does that look like and how do we measure such a love? If the offering of certain amounts of money and time are not the yardstick, then what is? Very simply, a hunger for Him and an inwardly growing revelation of who He is and who we are in the light of Him. David also wrote in Psalm 51 that God desires *"truth in our innermost being"*. Again, it must be emphasized that God does not desire that we possess merely doctrinal truth about Him, but a heart-knowledge of Him!

The question comes to mind, "Why should this sort of 'heart-knowledge' and worship be considered a sacrifice? After all, we're speaking of gentle Jesus, the sweet Lamb of God. What could possibly be costly in seeking after Him?" Very simply, there is a radical difference between understanding the precepts of God's holiness and actually experiencing it. But, that surely leads to an equally valid question: "I know I'm saved, because I asked Christ into my heart by faith. Are you trying to suggest that somehow I don't know God?" Not at all. But we so often possess little more than a very superficial knowledge of Him.

Perhaps the easiest way to illustrate the lack of depth we allow in our relationship with God is to consider a marriage which has completely lost the romance factor. The couple in the marriage may still be deeply committed to one another, just as we may have a deep sense of commitment to our Lord Jesus. The couple may be a very "righteous" couple – they would never cheat on one another, or lie to one another – just like Christians who know the Bible and understand what is the correct moral and ethical way to conduct their lives. The couple could be very hard-working and responsible, just as many Christians out of their commitment to God may give generously of their time and money. But the two vital things that first brought the couple together can be very dormant – *deep friendship and romance*. The absence of romance does not mean that they are not still committed to one another, and for sure they are still married legally speaking. In the same way, our simple belief in God and faith in our justification by the cross brings us into the Kingdom of

God. But, the hunger for God's Presence can be long gone. An individual, or even a church, which has lost the fervency for the person of Jesus, like a passionless marriage will come to the same point David's wife Michael did – *barrenness*.

> *"I know your deeds, your hard work and your perseverance. I know that you cannot tolerate wicked men, that you have tested those who claim to be apostles but are not, and have found them false. You have persevered and have endured hardships for my name, and have not grown weary. Yet I hold this against you: You have forsaken your first love. Remember the height from which you have fallen! Repent and do the things you did at first. If you do not repent, I will come to you and remove your lampstand from its place."*
>
> (Revelation 2:2–5 NIV)

Chapter 8

The Refining Fire of God

When we picture such a marriage as outlined at the end of the previous chapter, it might bring to mind a married couple you personally know. It might even represent your own marital situation, or that of your parents. Hopefully not. But as we picture such a couple, we can imagine the outward respectability; the years of faithfulness they've persevered through, remarkable by today's standards. Possibly we picture their nice house in a nice suburb where they are respected by neighbors and friends alike. Possibly, you work with someone who has a marriage like this and they are considered good, reliable, decent and hard working – respected by their peers. Yet, there seems to be something that is missing, something that makes marriage and life deeply fulfilling – *passion*. I'm not writing simply about emotionalism or outward signs of affection, but rather the pull of the heart towards their lover that both transcends and outweighs the normal joys and experiences of life.

When we read in the Bible of the putting on or taking off of clothing, usually the context has little to do with sensuality and more to do with conveying a sense of transparency before God. Such as when Adam and Eve grew estranged from God due to sin and their first response was to "cover up". Or, an opposite example, when Jesus at the Last Supper stripped down to a towel wrapped around Him in order to wash His disciples' feet. He was giving them a final lesson before the cross about who He truly was. He was powerfully demonstrating with both actual and symbolic transparency

His heart – the heart of a servant. Equally, in a healthy marriage a couple's ability to be naked together represents far more than mere physical intimacy, but a desire to be totally vulnerable and transparent with one another. In a healthy marriage the husband or wife is the one person that above all others, their mate can be totally open, transparent and vulnerable with – not just physically, but heart-to-heart as well.

John the Baptist called himself a "friend of the Bridegroom" because he understood his life's work was to help prepare a passionate bride for the Bridegroom of all bridegrooms. In the same vein Paul wrote to the church of Ephesus,

> *"For this reason a man will leave his father and mother and be united to his wife, and the two will become one flesh. This is a profound mystery – but I am talking about Christ and the church."*   (Ephesians 5:31–32 NIV)

Just as a very healthy marriage is rooted not only in commitment, but also in friendship and romance, so is our relationship with God to be. Unfortunately however, many Christians and congregations have never moved beyond the commitment stage into actual friendship and romance with God.

Friendship and romance with the Father

The romance and friendship in a healthy marriage is often visible in part, to others. It can be seen by friends, sometimes by how a couple look at one another with warmth and gentleness. It can be seen when they walk down the street hand in hand. It can be seen when they sit down on a couch their bodies support each other. It can be heard in the way they speak to one another with warmth and deference. For that couple the romance factor is often even stronger than when they first began to be serious about each other – even if it was years ago. But the deepest part of the intimacy cannot be seen publicly. It is what takes place as they are sharing their deep fears, dreams, and joys in private conversation. It is what takes place as they make love together in the sacredness of their bedroom. Often you get such a glimpse of a deep love for God when you see someone simply lost in devotion to God during a good worship service, or when out to lunch with a Christian friend the conversation changes from almost anything else to the topic of the person of the Lord Jesus – all of a sudden their eyes light up and they become much more animated, reluctant to want to change the subject. But what you cannot see is the vulnerability in their hearts and souls when they are praying and/or worshipping God. At times you get faint glimpses as they may be weeping before the Lord or simply caught up in the singing of a simple chorus that obviously has a significant meaning to them personally. The song they are singing might be the vehicle God is using to speak something fresh to them. Or it may be merely that that song, or chorus, might bring strong memories of a specific meeting with God, or a special insight the Lord gave them years ago. Those experiences are no different than when a couple who have been married for years and are still passionately in love, want to celebrate their 20th wedding anniversary by going back to the same hotel and resort area where they spent their honeymoon.

Just as there is an inner-strength of joy evident in the life of someone with passionate marriage, so it is visible with a lover of God. The secret for both is choosing to live in a sacred relationship of vulnerability, trust and transparency. And for that there simply is no substitute. They choose to live in a relationship of sacrificial love – not merely the sacrifice of gifts representing money and time to their spouse. After all, most of us probably know of marriages where costly gifts are given, but the heart of the marriage is bankrupt! A couple who are completely in love continually give the sacrificial love that only true lovers desire – more of themselves!

The gift of "more" – this is what God is after. Not our money and good works – although those sacrifices are the fruit of loving God – but, the sweet perfume of our hearts!

What is it actually that our hearts have that is of interest to God? Our hearts are the core of our being, the sun of the solar system of our lives. Proverbs 4:23 says,

*"Watch over your heart with all diligence,
for from it flow the springs of life."*   (NASB)

The milieu of all our life's many activities are governed by our hearts in much the same way that the planets rotate around the sun. The things we care about the most are the areas where we burn with the most energy. The things we do that are not close to our hearts, don't receive nearly so much energy, care and passion. We may intellectually value a person or a thing, but if we don't actually put time and energy into that person, or thing, then it's not really a priority of our hearts.

What God is after is that the sun of our solar systems – our hearts – to burn for Him. He is a God who, first and foremost, is desirous of a deep personal relationship – a relationship with a transparency like Adam and Eve had before the fall. The truth is that the whole world, whether they personally call on Jesus or not, is desperate for relationship with God. Non-believers might be totally ignorant of the gospel, or even the name of Christ, yet there is a universal hunger for true a heart-to-heart relationship without fear of rejection or condemnation.

The apostle John explained that God's perfect, or whole, love casts out all fear, because in His love, as expressed through Christ on the cross, there is never again a need to fear rejection, or condemnation. It is generally the fear of rejection due to shame, past failure and hurt, that prevents most people from really reaching out for what they need the most – unconditional love and acceptance. And even though by the blood of the Lamb, Christians have complete access to the "throne of Grace", many end up covering up just as Adam and Eve did, with religious actions and behavior. Thus, we can have all sorts of traditions and activities during our prayer and worship times, but God still seems aloof because we are really only covering up what He wants the most – our hearts! Draw near to God, the apostle James encourages us, and God will draw near to you!

We see evidence of humanity's cry for this unconditional love manifest in myriad ways. We see and hear it in the popular movies and songs. We see it in the desire of athletes to be the very best in order to win the respect and admiration of others – only to lose their own self-respect when their performance begins to slip. We see it as people constantly change their style of clothes, or speech, in order to fit in with a new peer group. We see it in bondage to pornography – a shallow, artificial, demeaning intimacy, but a hunger for intimacy nonetheless. Perhaps a person addicted to pornography is the most helpful example in trying to understand just how polluted and perverted the cry for intimacy can become when it is not focused on God.

It was God, the Creator of humanity, who made us with the inherent hunger for His perfect love. To step completely into that perfect love is much more than a "decision" made in response to a call from a preacher to "pray the sinner's prayer". That is only an initial "handshake" with the Lord Jesus Christ compared to the depth of relationship He really desires for us! He does not want to merely to free us from the grasp of hell, but rather, teach us to live, walk, and breath in Him. And that calls for daily sacrifice. God is after a day-in, day-out, sacrificial love for Him.

If we marry our doctrine and theology with an experiential knowledge of God, we find the experience of meeting with the Great I Am just as life-changing as the theology itself. After all, why did the apostle John on the Isle of Patmos fall face down, as a dead man while experiencing a fresh revelation of Jesus? Wasn't he one of the three disciples that, along with James and Peter, had seen Jesus transformed into glory decades before? Wasn't he one of the disciples that probably was closest to the Lord Jesus? Surely, he was the one who used to lean his head against Jesus' breast. Hadn't he, along with Peter and James, gone further into the Garden with Jesus than the other twelve? And after all, hadn't he seen just about everything there was to see in the explosion of the gospel in the nations for the next several decades after that great day of Pentecost? What was it that caused him to fall on his face at that revelation on Patmos? Simply, it was a greater revelation that he had previously experienced of the glory of the Lord. He lived the life that the apostle Paul wrote of in going from "glory to glory".

What many are too used to in contemporary congregations is an endless cycle of preaching, teaching and programs. All these may be centered around the truth of God, and they may be full of good intentions. But, just the same, they can also be devoid of the very presence of God. Let us seek after the Person of God and experience the fullness of "glory to glory" living that John did.

The throne zone

If God is after an ever-increasing, passionate heart-knowledge of Him personally, then we must press in to what I call the "throne zone" – the resting place of His Glory.

To approach the throne of God, we must learn for ourselves first-hand the lessons the Levites learned in approaching the Holy of Holies. When they first entered the gates into the outer courts they were confronted with the Burnt Offering Altar and then the Laver. At the Altar of Burnt Offering was where offerings were sacrificed by fire. It was here where the Levites would come to provide a sacrifice without blemish – the very best available. The blood of the offering was, as part of the process, poured out around the altar.

The sacrifice of perfect, spotless male animals was symbolic of the eternal sacrifice of Jesus, the Lamb of God, which was still to come. Luke tells us in his gospel account that as Jesus, the sacrificial Lamb of God, was being offered on the cross as payment for our sins that *"the sun was darkened, and the veil of the temple was rent in the midst"*. When the Levites offered up their sacrifices at the Altar of Burnt Offering, smoke would fill the Tent of Meeting. For Jesus on the cross it was most certainly His darkest hour. In His obedience to the Father, as the sin of the world came upon Him, the eternal fellowship of the Father left Him. For the first time ever, He was bereft of the Father's surrounding and empowering love. It was a time of darkness inwardly, and outwardly, for Jesus. But, immediately the veil which separated the Holy of Holies from the Holy Place was rent in two.

> *"At that moment the curtain of the temple was torn in two from top to bottom. The earth shook and the rocks split."*
> (Matthew 27:51 NIV)

To go from the Holy Place into the actual glory of God, always calls for sacrifice. And although, our sins were fully paid for by the once for all sacrifice of the blood of the Lamb, Jesus, God is still looking for the sacrifice of brokenness to become evident in our lives.

Although the Bible does not give us the dimensions of every item of furniture and ornament within the temple, it would seem that the Altar of Burnt Offering was by far the most imposing piece. This is significant, for it symbolizes the fact that the truly essential thing for each one of us as we come to God, is to embrace the person of Jesus and understand the great sacrifice that He made as the Lamb of God.

The fire of the Burnt Offering Altar was basic, foundational, essential cleansing. It is symbolic of the forgiveness of sins, as well as of the "dying to self" that we should experience when we surrender our lives to Jesus. The cleansing at the Laver of the feet and hands, is symbolic of the necessary and ongoing *washing away* of the "dirt" that, in spiritual terms, we encounter in life. For example, Jesus told His disciples when He cleansed their feet at the Last Supper, *"A person who has had a bath needs only to wash his feet; his whole body is clean"*. It was a surface cleansing they were experiencing. The fire of the Altar of Burnt Offering however, was much deeper.

As the Laver had to do with the outward and the superficial, the Burnt Offering Altar had to do with the inward and the heart-condition. Consider the difference between repenting over some sin we committed in the last week, and a repentance that seeks to address the issue of who we are inside that causes us to commit the sin. David wrote in Psalm 27 that both *clean hands* and a *pure heart* are required to ascend the hill of the Lord. Jesus stated in the sermon on the mount that only those with a pure heart would see God.

Why did Paul make a point of telling his readers that, "many among you are weak and sick, and a number of you have fallen asleep", attributing their afflictions to the fact that they were partaking of the bread and wine of communion in an unworthy manner? Because he knew that they were missing the point of the sacrament and were treating it with superficiality. How many of us take communion without really examining our hearts? Why is it that so many Christians endlessly repent of the sins they have committed, but keep falling back into the same old patterns? It is because they have never really embraced the cross or visited the Altar of Burnt Offering. Many have circumvented the Fire of God and opted for the surface cleansing of the Laver, which temporarily refreshes, but never burns away the flesh. I'm not referring simply to loud and emotional outward displays as a sign of true repentance, although such signs may often accompany true repentance. I'm speaking of a deep regret inwardly in our hearts – a brokenness not only over what we've done, but who we really are – our inward drives and motivations, revealed only in the light of His Presence.

We are usually very aware of the "outer sins" in our lives, but the deep, ongoing sins of our hearts, such as pride, envy, bitterness, jealousy, etc., are not so much self-discerned, but rather revealed by the Holy Spirit. As Jeremiah said,

> *"The heart is deceitful above all things and beyond cure. Who can understand it? 'I the LORD search the heart'"*
> (Jeremiah 17:9–10 NIV)

The New Testament invitation to embrace the fire of the Burnt Offering Altar is found in Revelation 3:18 where Jesus declares,

> *"I counsel you to buy from me gold refined in the fire, so you can become rich."*

Although that verse is popularly quoted by evangelists when preaching to non-believers, Jesus was not addressing His remarks to that audience, He was inviting the Church to a deeper cleansing by the fire of God. The fire causes parts of our heart to be burnt away like a surgeon cutting away a cancer from one's body. The promised fruit is the only true wealth that will never rust, cannot be stolen, and will certainly never depreciate – Christ Himself!

Sometimes, the brokenness of the heart is a season which prepares us for a deeper revelation of God than we can handle right now. Sometimes, as with the sacrifice of our early morning prayer times, it leads us to an honesty in our hearts that acknowledges that we are not the center of our lives, but He is.

This sacrifice of a broken and contrite heart on our part, in no way renders the sacrifice of Jesus incomplete. Rather the sacrifice of Jesus gives us the grace, mercy and freedom in which to then offer our hearts to God. But, there will always be the cost of dying to self, if one is truly going to experience God's glory. Before the throne of God, the place where His Holiness and Glory dwells, there is absolutely no room for our pride, self-glory or ego. The Holy Place and the Holy of Holies cannot be entered into until the Laver and the Altar of Burnt Offering have been experienced.

All who have called on Jesus to be their Lord and Savior have entry into the Kingdom of God, but when we draw near to Him in Heaven, will we be near enough to attend to Him or be merely standing in the background? The cost of true intimacy with Him is choosing to die to self and becoming a worshipper in Spirit and in Truth. There are no substitutes. We can busy ourselves with religious traditions and behavior, but to die to self, ambition and monument building, and to be absorbed by Him, calls for death by choice under the guillotine of humility.

Fenelon, who was denounced by Pope Innocent XII for "having loved God too much, and man too little", wrote:

> "God, who wants to strip the soul to perfect it, and will pursue it relentlessly toward a purer love, makes it really pass these tests of itself, and does not let it rest until it has taken away all reversion and self-support from its love." *(Christian Perfection*, p. 149)

Fenelon, realized that although God wants to strip our hearts of all form of idolatry He limits Himself to pursuing us, leading us and guiding us. It is we ourselves who must choose to buy the gold refined by His fire. He will not force us to do so because love is always a choice. When the woman crashed the dinner party at Simon's house in Mark 14, she herself had to break her alabaster box of sweet perfume! Jesus would never have taken it from her except as a gift!

God longs for your and my heart to be broken and longing for Him, but He will not break it for us. Love is always a choice. The call on the Levites is to choose to move beyond the surface cleansing and embrace the costly consuming fire of His Glory! And like the parable of the invitations to the wedding feast, many are called but few are chosen!

The light of His Presence will cause our sins to be visible according to Psalm 90:8. It is at that point that we choose to enter into a mode of either repentance or rebellion. We choose to humble ourselves and repent of that which, up to this point in time, may have been covered over by ignorance, or we choose to hang on to our pride along with our pet idols. Samuel Rutherford, the famous Scottish minister of the 17th century wrote,

> "So narrow is the entry to heaven, that our knots, our bunches and lumps of pride, and self-love, and world-love, must be hammered off us, and we may throng in, stooping low, and creeping through that narrow and thorny entry."

The "hammering" Rutherford writes of can only effect-ively take place when we've allowed our hearts and souls to be softened in the crucible of His fire and glory. Up until that time it's as if our accomplishments, strengths and offerings to God and man, rise up like a fortified castle primarily serving to protect our frail self-identities. Outwardly we imagine castle walls of beautiful stonework and masonry rising up in Babylonian-type towers topped by colorful banners which display the unholy trinity of "Me, Myself, and I". On closer examination however, by the light of His presence, we see that those stones, rather than solid bricks, more closely resemble playing cards held tenuously held together with the weak glue of ego. When the wind of His Spirit blows the fire of His presence upon these "religious houses of card" they collapse and become consumed. Our garments of supposed excellence are burned away and our true nakedness is revealed.

But, if we dare to believe in His goodness we press on anyway. And, despite the heat, the fire, and the shame, we find the greatest place of all – the mercy seat – the resting place of His glory. And we find that if we have fallen on the rock, rather than waiting for the rock to fall on us, His righteousness becomes the eternal garment we put on – garments of pure white linen with which to cover our nakedness; His balm to heal our blindness; His peace and joy to replace our pain and fear.

Chapter 9

Where Are the Levites? (part 2)

On Nicole Nordeman's superb CD appropriately entitled *Wide Eyed*, there is a song called "Anyway". In this song she considers her life as a dusty, worn out picture in the Gallery of God. "No Michelangelo am I", she confesses. But, to her surprise and joy in encountering the master of the gallery she sings, "But, You called me beautiful, when You saw my shame. And You placed me on the wall, anyway"! This is precisely what we find when we choose to cast down our crown, both real and imagined, and press in on God. When we embrace the altar, the stones of fire surrounding the throne of God, before the Holy Place, and the presence of God at the Mercy Seat, we find love, acceptance, and healing!

Remember that there was a two-step process required of the Levites in the Outer Court before they could enter the Holy Place. First, was the cleansing of the Burnt Offering Altar – symbolic of repenting of what we are. After that came the Laver, or the washing of current or surface sins. Often we do honestly repent of things we have done which have been in rebellion towards God and hurtful towards others. However, if we are truly going to become the friends of God, and position ourselves to experience God's open heavens, then the requirement is more than simply regretting past mistakes. It requires the humility of no longer living for self. It necessitates the setting aside of the *childish*, self-centered cry "Me, Me, Me" in favor of *childlike*, simple obedience. It calls us to learn to be consumed with the all-consuming fire of He Himself. His absolute glory and majesty demands no less! But, if we will pass over the stones of fire, and allow the ugly cancers of ego and pride to be burned away, the reward is the greatest prize of all. He, the person of God, becomes our portion in the land of the living.

As we pass from the Outer Court into the Holy Place, we not only begin to see, but we begin to experience three things: The Showbread Table, the Lampstand, and Golden Incense altar. The Outer Court was a place of repentance, cleansing, darkness, and death. The Holy Place is a place of food, light, and sweetness – a place of abundant life. These three items were essential elements of the Temple Priest's service. Each had a special significance which can teach us about how we relate to the Father.

On the right-hand side after entering the Holy Place was the Showbread Table. It was made from acacia wood and overlaid with gold. The table itself had a crown of gold symbolic of the King of kings Himself, Jesus. On the table there could be found twelve loaves of bread – one for each of the twelve tribes. Although only the Levites were allowed to minister to the actual presence of the Lord, the benefits were for all Israel. Whenever God can find saints or spiritual Levites of the faith on the earth, who are committed to seeking His face, the grace of God is exponentially poured out on the church, even though their ministries may be completely hidden from man!

We need New Covenant Levites to emerge today. We desperately need to get back the *bread* of His Presence. Naomi, her husband Elimelech, and their two sons, left Judah and went to live in the land of Israel's enemies, the Moabites, because there was famine in the land. Many churches today are strong in their doctrines, programs and traditions, but have no food for spiritually starving people. As a result there has been an exodus in the last 30 years from the traditional church offered by western civilization. During those years we have seen a rapid increase in followers of false religions, the New Age movement, and the occult. Too many preachers stand Sunday after Sunday in their pulpits proclaiming the evil in the land. The problem however, is not so much the enemies of the Church, but the lack of fresh bread in the temple!

After her husband and two sons died, Naomi along with one of her two daughters-in-law, Ruth, returned to Israel because *"she had heard . . . that the Lord had visited His People in giving them food"* (Ruth 1:6 NASB). We can rant and rave about sin and sinners all we want, but until we have the food that they desperately need, why should they come running to the Church? It's not enough that we preach and teach. Jesus told people that if they could not believe purely on the basis of His words, then at least they should believe because of the miracles and great acts He did (John 14:11). We must have more than mere words today if we are truly going to see a great harvest. We need the freedom that only the Bread of Life Himself brings. People in this post-modern age are going to extremes to try to fill a void that only God can fill. If the church cannot offer the only true food that will satisfy their appetite for God, then people will go to the camp of the enemy in desperation.

Across from the Showbread Table, on the left-hand side of the Holy Place was the Lampstand. In contrast to the dark smoke of the Outer Court was the bright light in the Holy Place. The Lampstand was made out of a solid piece of pure gold, which was then shaped by being beaten. The Lampstand was shaped into seven branches like almond tree branches in blossom. The branches ended in bowls which contained oil that was replenished every morning and evening and burned continuously.

In the recent U2 song *When I look at the World*, singer/songwriter Bono, sings "Without you it's no use, I can't see what you see when I look at the world". There is an almost painful desperation voiced in these lyrics. The listener can easily sense his near-hopelessness to see things from a more true and more hopeful perspective. In Sue Rinaldi's song *Restless Pilgrim*, she sings "give me the eyes of a prophet – help me to see the unseen". *Restless Pilgrim* is a particularly poignant song that comes across much more like a heartcry than a worship song. These two artists, Bono and Rinaldi, move in two very different worlds. U2 has been one of the most prolific bands in the world of rock and pop music for almost two decades. While Rinaldi also tends to be cutting-edge in much of her music, her primary emphasis is more worship oriented and spiritual in focus. In both artists however, there is an equally passionate cry to see far beyond the skin and the human rationale that governs most vision. In both there is an equally identifiable longing that many can perhaps identify with. That longing is much like the longing of one who only sees in black and white, but has heard a rumor that somewhere there is color. There remains for the for the Church the apostle Paul's prayer of Ephesians 1:18, that *"the eyes of our hearts may be enlightened."* That enlightenment begins to become fulfilled as we learn to draw near to the light of His Presence. It is through learning to offer up the sweet sacrifice of prayer and praise which is incense to God, that we come into that clarity, even as the Levites would come into the light of the Golden Lamp in the Holy Place. It is in that place of holy fellowship and intimacy with God that Jesus heals our eyes so that we might truly see.

Often, as God takes us through the refiner's fire, we think the goal is simply to make us pure – i.e. having removed all our bad habits. But, holiness means far more than merely the absence of sin. The purity of the gold from which the Lampstand was made was just the starting place. After being refined it then had to be beaten into shape! Holiness, is much more than self-righteousness. True Holiness is to be *wholly set aside for God.* Our pride and human logic tell us that after laying down a habit that is displeasing to God, we are now ready and can get on with our ministry unhindered. But it is only after the refining fire that the real process of sanctification and consecration can begin as the beating of God starts to take affect on our character. Many, misunderstanding the necessity of the process of ongoing sanctification, mistakenly think God has abandoned them, or that they must be committing some awful sin unwittingly, as they experience wilderness experiences. It's so hard for us to really understand that God does not want to merely set us free from sin and hell, He wants to make us into the image and likeness of His Son, Jesus. He wants to form us into a vessel that can truly carry the precious oil of the Holy Spirit. God's method of fashioning such vessels is so completely alien to the wisdom of man. Man's way of achieving things involves building himself up to become strong. God's way, in startling contrast, is to empty Man and break him so that He can fill him with His Spirit!

It is only by dying to self and becoming Christ-like that we can really become carriers of the Holy Spirit. We must learn to recognize our need of continually being filled with the Holy Spirit as the Bible describes it. Many Christians burn brightly for a while but then fail to stay that "light set on a hill" because they refuse to allow the strong but loving discipline of the Father to continue to shape them. They run for a while in their enthusiasm, but never go from being a single flicker to a fully-fledged carrier of His light and fire. They may even go through periodic cleansings at the Laver. The prophet or evangelist may come to their church and give a call to holiness to which they'll respond. But unless they go from the Laver – the place of superficial cleansing – on to the Altar of Burnt Offerings, they will never arrive at the Holy Place. It was this realization that caused Isaiah the prophet, when beholding the glory of the Lord, to cry out,

> *"Woe is me! for I am undone ... for mine eyes have seen the King, the* Lord *of hosts."*   (Isaiah 6:5 KJV)

Isaiah wasn't repenting of an issue of sin in his life, he had realized that God's holiness demanded his entire life be unraveled in order to remake him into a messenger of the Lord.

How many priests, prophets, pastors, teachers and evangelists today give us words about God, and even from God, but fail to be carriers of the light and glory of God? If we are to become true Levites – carriers of God's glory – then – there can be no half measures. We must allow the deep dealings of God within us so that we might truly be vessels of the fire and light of His presence to those around us.

The branches of the Lampstand were fashioned so as to resemble an almond tree in a time of blossom. The almond tree symbolizes the fact that we will bear fruit when we are in the will and presence of God. We tend to be most productive when we are truly focused on the task at hand. If the eyes of our hearts are primarily focused on the Person of God, then we will produce godliness in abundance. Any preoccupation with things other than God Himself, will produce less than that.

The branches of almond trees in the Bible also depict waiting on God or seeking His face. God used the image in order to speak to Jeremiah:

> *"The word of the* LORD *came to me: 'What do you see, Jeremiah?' 'I see the branch of an almond tree,' I replied. The* LORD *said to me, 'You have seen correctly, for I am watching to see that my word is fulfilled.'"*
> (Jeremiah 1:11–12 NIV)

Here the almond tree represents waiting and watching to see what the Lord will do. The Hebrew word for almond is *shaqed* (pronounced shaw-kade). *Shaqed* is derived from the Hebrew word which means "to be sleepless, to remain, to watch and be alert". We are so used to the "noise" of our churches programs that we've all but lost the art of waiting on the Lord and seeking His face. I believe a key word for the contemporary church is Psalm 46:10:

> *"Be still, and know that I am God;*
> *I will be exalted among the nations,*
> *I will be exalted in the earth."*

We are called to serve the Lord with energy and enthusiasm, but perhaps the most difficult assignment for God's people is to wait on Him and learn what He is doing. It's so easy to become totally consumed with what we are doing for Jesus that we lose sight of what Jesus Himself is doing. We should be consumed with Jesus! True transformation of our inner beings will only come by spending time with God, learning to fully devote our hearts to Him. Just as the facial expressions of newborn babies imitate the face of the one they look at the most, so we must fix our gaze upon Jesus and become more like Him. Then we will change from glory to glory and break free from the cycle of endless religious repetition! We are quick to justify our worth by our endless tasks for the Lord, but never see the great harvest we desire until we have more of Christ in our lives and His life overflows us to touch others. Nevertheless, we must stifle the endless noise of our own thinking, plotting and planning and learn, as Mary did, to just sit at His feet in adoration.

There is a level of fruitfulness that only spending time alone with God will produce. Ruth Ward Heflin, the well-known speaker/author on revival, prayer and the glory of God, is credited with the following.

> "There is a greater change that comes about through worship than through any other means. If you want to be changed, worship is the key. When you are worshipping you look into His face, and you are changed from glory to glory. We become like that which we worship. We become like Him whom we worship."

Lastly, after passing between the Lampstand and the Showbread Table the priest would come to the Golden Incense Altar. Like the Showbread Table, the Incense Altar had a golden crown running all along the top edge symbolizing the Kingship of Jesus. The Incense Altar served as a final threshold before the veil which separated the Holy of Holies from the Holy Place. The sweet-smelling Incense Altar symbolizes the sweetness of life that can only be realized by experiencing intimacy with the Father. David, in Psalm 16 wrote:

> *"You have made known to me the path of life;*
> *you will fill me with joy in your presence,*
> *with eternal pleasures at your right hand."*
>   (Psalm 16:11 NIV)

To help us compare the quality of life which flows from the very presence of God, to that which abounds in the Church today, we can examine the comparison between "heavenly" and "earthly" food as found in C.S. Lewis' book *Perelandra*. It is a fictional account of a man who, assisted by angelic beings, travels to Venus. Venus in the story, is a planet which has never experienced sin, or the great fall, which the earth has. The following paragraph describes that man's experience of eating his first bite of food in this unspoiled realm.

"He had meant to extract the smallest, experimental sip, but the first taste put his caution all to flight. It was, of course, a taste, just as his thirst and hunger had been thirst and hunger. But then it was so different from every other taste that it seemed mere pedantry to call it a taste at all. It was like the discovery of a totally new genus of pleasures, something unheard of among men, out of all reckoning, beyond all covenant. For one draught of this on earth wars would be fought and nations betrayed. It could not be classified and he could never tell us, when he came back to the world of men, whether it was sharp or sweet, savory or voluptuous, creamy or piercing. 'Not like that' was all he could ever say to such inquires." [1]

In a great marriage, or friendship, we can experience a glimpse of what it is like to experience God's unconditional love in an intimate relationship with Him. When we see spectacular scenery such as the Grand Canyon, or Niagara Falls, we get a vague glimpse of God's glory. These glorious creations, however, pale in comparison to the glory of the Creator Himself. When we really begin to continuously imbibe the sweet incense of God's presence, we in turn burn so much more intensely. True God-addicts, in turn, always go on to impart a hunger to both the Church and the lost to also taste and see the goodness of God. John Wesley, the great English revivalist, when asked how to start a revival replied,

"I light myself on fire for God, collect a crowd, and let them watch me burn."

The symbolism of the Golden Incense Altar is probably the most difficult for us to understand and accept. We can maybe come to terms with the fact that God needs to cleanse and purify us; that He needs to transform and mold our characters. What is harder to comprehend is that God really delights in us, and desires for us to delight in Him also. If we could walk in continuous revelation of what the grace of God extended to us through the cross has really accomplished, then such afflictions as loneliness, fear and rejection, would begin to have absolutely no meaning whatsoever in our personal lexicons – they would have no power to manipulate! What the cross has accomplished is the total separation of our confessed sins, as far from us as the East is from the West. Because of the Lamb of God we are completely acceptable to the Father. Therefore, He requires that we begin to move, breath, and abide in a context of loving Him and receiving love from Him. He desires that just as He has given us the best He has to offer – Jesus – that we give Him the best we have to offer – our hearts in worship.

If we consider ourselves or one another from a pharisaical viewpoint, judging our own failures, inadequacies and idiosyncrasies, it is so difficult to imagine God placing a high value on the songs we sing and the prayers we pray. But, the Bible tells us that He receives them like a sweet and fragrant aroma, as the apostle John revealed during his awesome revelation of the throne room of God.

> *"And I saw the seven angels who stand before God, and to them were given seven trumpets. Another angel, who had a golden censer, came and stood at the altar. He was given much incense to offer, with the prayers of all the saints, on the golden altar before the throne. The smoke of the incense, together with the prayers of the saints, went up before God from the angel's hand. Then the angel took the censer, filled it with fire from the altar, and hurled it on the earth, and there came peals of thunder, rumblings, flashes of lightning and an earthquake."* (Revelation 8:2–5 NIV)

As we read these words of John we grasp the idea that God's purposes for our prayers and worship are far more than we realize or imagine. They are not a religious exercise designed to make us feel better. The Father takes very, very seriously the sacrifice of His only begotten Son, Jesus. It stands to reason that He takes us, His adopted sons and daughters, very seriously too. He takes great notice of the prayers and worship we offer up to His throne. This passage in Revelation seems to indicate that He may even allow us to partner with Him in releasing both blessings and judgments on the world around us.

The Levitical priests who served in the Holy Place would twice daily, in the morning and evening, burn incense at the altar. When we pray, even though our prayers may feel weak in the face of great difficulties and problems, our high priest Jesus is adding incense to our prayers. He is making them not only acceptable to the Father, but even sweet to Him.

When we closely examine the revelation contained in biblical prophecy from prophets such as John and Daniel, we see that by far the overwhelming activity we see taking place around the throne of God is *worship*. The angels, cherubim and seraphim, the elders of Israel – the only thing they can do when in the very presence of Almighty God is to worship Him.

It was at the precise second when Lucifer began to be more interested in his own beauty than in his appointed function as the chief of the worshipping angels that he was thrown down from the presence of God. He was no longer qualified to be in God's immediate presence because he had ceased to be a worshipper (Ezekiel 28:12–17). He himself had become the center of his universe.

Satan's downfall was pride, and pride is usually Man's chief dilemma also. Who will we worship, God or ourselves, the Creator or the creation? Who, or what are we going to give our hearts and beings to? Either it will be God, or it won't be God, because no man can serve two masters. It will either be God, or self, but not both. This is why Jesus said the Father is searching for those who will worship Him in Spirit as well as in Truth. This is our high calling – to minister to God. And this is why today, the call is going forth from the Holy Spirit to the Church, "Where are the Levites?" Because without them, without a people who according to biblical patterns will set themselves aside exclusively for the fire and person of God, who then will be the carriers of His glory?

When David went a second time to attempt to bring the Ark into the City of David, he did two things differently from the first time. Firstly, he did not allow the Ark to be put on a new cart, no matter how elaborate that cart may have been.

He went back to the God-ordained way of transporting the Ark – he made the Levites carry it! In 2 Chronicles 15 we read the following:

> *"Then David summoned Zadok and Abiathar the priests, and Uriel, Asaiah, Joel, Shemaiah, Eliel and Amminadab the Levites. He said to them, 'You are the heads of the Levitical families, you and your fellow Levites are to consecrate yourselves and bring up the ark of the LORD, the God of Israel, to the place I have prepared for it. It was because you, the Levites, did not bring it up the first time that the LORD our God broke out in anger against us. We did not inquire of him about how to do it in the prescribed way.' So the priests and Levites consecrated themselves in order to bring up the ark of the LORD, the God of Israel. And the Levites carried the ark of God with the poles on their shoulders, as Moses had commanded in accordance with the word of the LORD."*
> (1 Chronicles 15:11–15 NIV)

The second thing that David did differently was that he and Israel worshipped God with an expensive and extravagant sacrifice. As they sang and danced while the Levites carried the Ark, they stopped every six paces and sacrificed an oxen as a burnt offering. Experts tell us that the distance from the home of Obed-Edom, where the Ark had been, to the City of David was somewhere between seven and thirteen miles. Even if we take the median distance, say ten miles, they must have sacrificed close to 3000 oxen with fire. In terms of cost, it must have been the equivalent value of a modern-day, $30,000 dollar tractor to a farmer. It was costly both in terms of money and energy to bring in the Ark of God. If you could have stood at the end of the dirt road at the City of David and looked back on the whole 10 miles, it would look like a road of dirt and blood, continuously. This is the picture of the road up Calvary Hill when Jesus carried the cross. The dirt of the road, the sweat and pain of His labor, the road spattered by the blood from the beatings, the whippings, and the crown of thorns He had received. Finally Man's own dirt – our sin – came upon Him. This was an extravagant display by the Father of His love for us. There is absolutely nothing else of comparative value that the Father could have given us as a sign of His great heart for us. Romans 8:32 says,

> *"He* [the Father] *who did not spare his own Son, but gave him up for us all – how will he not also, along with him, graciously give us all things?"*

The Lamb of God is the eternal gift of all the universe!

Far and wide, the theme of revival and a great harvest has been preached, taught, prayed and prophesied for the last several years. But, until the Church learns to seek the Lord of revival rather than the event itself; until we learn to delight in the Creator rather than merely creation; until we learn to gaze on the gift-Giver instead of hungering for the gifts, we will fall short of the fullness of what God has for our generations. It will not be until we embrace the cleansing water and holy fire of the Outer Court that we can enter the Holy Place. And it will not be till we learn to live in the light of His presence and to eat of the Bread Himself, and to offer up a sweet smell to our King, that we can really press on to the higher call of experiencing more of His Kingdom on earth as it is in Heaven.

Note

1.   C.S. Lewis, *Perelandra*, Macmillan, p. 42.

Chapter 10

Restoring the Tabernacle of David

In the previous chapter we looked briefly at two things King David did differently in his second, and successful attempt at bringing in the Ark of God into the City. I would now like to discuss, two totally unique things regarding the Tabernacle of David, in comparison to the Tabernacle of Moses, and of the later Kings of Israel, and what they may suggest prophetically for the Church today.

In the book of Amos we read these prophetic words:

> " 'In that day I will restore David's fallen tent. I will repair its broken places, restore its ruins, and build it as it used to be, so that they may possess the remnant of Edom and all the nations that bear my name,' declares the LORD, who will do these things. 'The days are coming,' declares the LORD, 'when the reaper will be overtaken by the plowman and the planter by the one treading grapes. New wine will drip from the mountains and flow from all the hills.' "
>
> (Amos 9:11–13 NIV)

In Acts 15:16–17, the apostle Peter quotes Amos' prophecy in his speech to the rest of the elders and apostles in Jerusalem, as he addresses the issue of the Gospel spreading amongst the Gentiles.

> " 'After this I will return and rebuild David's fallen tent. Its ruins I will rebuild, and I will restore it, that the remnant of

men may seek the Lord, and all the Gentiles who bear my name,' says the Lord, who does these things."

One of the intriguing things about biblical prophecy is that it is often multifaceted in its application and meaning. It has a primary meaning and application for its recipients at the time it is given, but can also have a different application for others at a later date. The classic example of this is the prophecy contained in the book of Revelation. The apostle John had seven specific prophetic words from the Lord Jesus for seven churches. Those words were very much for the seven churches of that day, but they also have a tremendous application for the contemporary Church.

Another example is found in the book of Joel. We know that on the day of Pentecost Peter quoted Joel's prophecy about the Spirit of God being poured out on all of mankind. "This is that which Joel prophesied!" Peter proclaimed. He claimed the prophecy as solid biblical evidence for what appeared to the critics to be mere drunkenness induced by wine. Yet, with the benefit of some two thousand years of history since Pentecost, we could say that Joel's prophecy has still not been completely fulfilled. We have still not seen the Spirit of God touch "all of mankind" as Joel predicted in the prophecy (Joel 2:28). That same prophetic word gives us hope today of an increased harvest among all peoples.

I believe the Holy Spirit can use such prophecies as Joel's and Amos' to have a significant meaning for many different generations throughout church history. In a very real sense David's Tent, or Tabernacle, was restored in two different ways through the person of Jesus. Firstly, the glory of God became known to the world through Jesus the Messiah, the Savior of Humanity. And secondly, just as we read that there was no veil in David's tabernacle, so when Jesus died on the cross, the veil which hung in the temple separating the Holy of Holies from the rest of the Temple was torn in two. In Christ Jesus all the barriers between Man and God are torn apart.

I believe that these prophecies have a prophetic application for the Church today. I believe the Holy Spirit is shining a spotlight onto the contemporary Church and is calling for

Her to "rebuild" David's tabernacle in many differing ways, shapes and forms at this time. What does this mean?

Let's look at 1 Chronicles 16:1–6 and examine what stands out between David's Tabernacle and that of Moses and later, Solomon:

> *"They brought the ark of God and set it inside the tent that David had pitched for it, and they presented burnt offerings and fellowship offerings before God. After David had finished sacrificing the burnt offerings and fellowship offerings, he blessed the people in the name of the LORD. Then he gave a loaf of bread, a cake of dates and a cake of raisins to each Israelite man and woman. He appointed some of the Levites to minister before the ark of the LORD, to make petition, to give thanks, and to praise the LORD, the God of Israel: Asaph was the chief, Zechariah second, then Jeiel, Shemiramoth, Jehiel, Mattithiah, Eliab, Benaiah, Obed-Edom and Jeiel. They were to play the lyres and harps, Asaph was to sound the cymbals, and Benaiah and Jahaziel the priests were to blow the trumpets regularly before the ark of the covenant of God."*

The first thing that really stands out when comparing David's Tabernacle and the others is the lack of a veil. Argument by silence is usually not iron clad. However, the Bible takes care to describe in detail the construction of such items, and the fact that there is no mention of a veil in David's Tabernacle is significant.

In the description of both the Tent of Moses and later the Temple of Solomon the veil is discussed and very much stands out as an important feature. Exodus chapter 26 contains the directions given by God to Moses for making the Tent of Meeting to house the Ark. In verses 31–33 we read the directions for the manufacture and use of the "curtain" or veil. According to verse 33 the primary function of this veil was to *"separate the Holy Place from the Most Holy Place"* where the Ark was. And again in Exodus 40:3 we read, *"Place the ark of the Testimony in it and shield the ark with the curtain."* Similarly, we read in 2 Chronicles 3:14 of Solomon having an elaborate curtain made to hang between the Ark with the Cherubim and the Holy Place. Such a veil is conspicuous by its absence in the description of David's Tabernacle.

Why is this significant? Because it speaks of the accessibility to the presence of God that is now available to every one of us through the Lord Jesus Christ. It represents the truth that God is inviting us to come into the very Holy of Holies to worship Him.

Why would God then want to restore, in a symbolic sense, the Tent of David and not of Moses or Solomon? And why should we want God to do such a thing? Because David's life represented the all-consuming passion for God of a true worshipper. David was always more than a king, a warrior, or even an artist. First and foremost he was a worshipper and a lover of God. He was a man with a "heart after God". This is the man who had everything he could ever want within his grasp as king. Yet, he sang in one of his many love songs to God,

> *"One thing I ask of the* LORD,
>   *this is what I seek:*
> *that I may dwell in the house of the* LORD
>   *all the days of my life,*
> *to gaze upon the beauty of the* LORD
>   *and to seek him in his temple."*   (Psalm 27:4 NIV)

Many will remember the great line spoken by the crusty trail-hardened cowboy in the movie *City Slickers* to the wannabe cowboy played by Billy Crystal. He is trying to give some advice about finding true fulfillment in life to Billy Crystal's character who's a middle-aged New Yorker in the midst of a full-blown mid-life crisis. The old weather-beaten cowboy declares authoritatively "You've gotta find that one thing that makes all of life worthwhile." When Billy Crystal, with eager anticipation asks the cowboy "What is the one thing?" he replies, to Billy's great disappointment, "I don't know, that's for you to find out!"

David had found his "one thing" in the presence of God. More than his personal glory, power or wealth he wanted to gaze on the glory of God. This is why David's Tent, as opposed to the incredible opulence of Solomon's, or the historical one of Moses, was what pleased God most. And that Tent is a picture of how God desires us to relate to Him today. It represents the kind of relationship that Adam and Eve enjoyed with God in the Garden before the fall – where neither God nor Man had any need for curtains, clothing or hiding.

God is longing to meet with His people in true intimacy. He is longing for a people who want to sit down and "dine with Him" (Revelation 3:20); a people who will worship Him as David did, in Spirit and in Truth; a people who are seeking His face of glory more than His hand of blessing. His promise found in James 4–8 is still true. If we will draw near to God He will draw near to us. The question is where are the people who will pursue Him more than His things?

The second significant thing that stands out about the Tent of Meeting that David established was regular, or continual worship. What followed the construction of Moses' tabernacle was the Law. What stands out in 1 Kings chapter six, as it describes the building of Solomon's temple, is the expensive materials used and the extravagant design and workmanship. It was seven years in the making. But what God was ultimately after was neither man's self-righteousness nor an expensive attempt tot make something big and beautiful for Him. Rather, He simply wanted, as He does today, love, worship and relationship. He wanted a people who would be known by Him and know Him – a people who would delight in Him far more than His things or His gifts.

As it was then, so it is today. God is not after a people who think they can stand before Him on the basis on their own performance. Neither is He at all impressed by our great sacrifices. The one whom He will look to, according to Isaiah the prophet is the one *"who is humble and contrite in spirit, and trembles at my word"* (Isaiah 66:2 NIV). This only ones who can truly make a resting place for God are people who are desperate for Him!

The heart of David was one of a deep, life-long, un-quenchable passion for God. The Tabernacle he built was nothing spectacular to look on. Neither was it followed by a revelation of the Law such as with Moses. Rather it simply represented an unabashed love for God and His presence.

1 Chronicles chapter 9 gives us an insight into the number of Levite Priests who King David and Samuel the Prophet appointed to care for the *"house of the Lord – the house called the Tent"* (1 Chronicles 9:23 NIV). The responsibilities of the Priests were greatly varied. Some prepared the incense offered up to the Lord. Others baked the bread used for the "Showbread". Verse 33 however, tells us that there were *"musicians, heads of Levite families, [who] stayed in the rooms of the temple and were exempt from other duties because they were responsible for the work day and night."* The inference seems clear – if there was not actually 24-hour-a-day worship, then it was close to it!

So, besides the probable lack of a veil, probably the most noteworthy fact about David's Tent was its continuous worship. Whether that worship was 24-hours a day or not, we cannot say for sure, but there was certainly regular, passionate worship going on before the Tent of Glory, probably on a night and day schedule. While it is true that Solomon did have worship at the dedication of the Temple he built (2 Chronicles 6 & 7), it is only in the description of David's Tent that we read *"the priests were to blow the trumpets regularly before the ark of the covenant of God"* (1 Chronicles 16:6 NIV). The word "regularly" is the NIV translation of the Hebrew word *tamiyd* which basically means a constant or perpetual continuation. It is possible, perhaps even probable, that David did establish 24-hour-a-day worship, but at the very least it's safe to say that several times a day worship of the Lord God Jehovah was taking place, which is quite different from what either Moses or Solomon established.

Perhaps the third thing that really stands out from 1 Chronicles 16 is the fact that the continual worship was *"before the ark of ... God."* The worship David established was totally, one hundred percent meant for God's enjoyment! All too often churches today when considering issues relating to worship are mainly concerned with ministering to man. Either we are worried about breaking with tradition and offending people or we are concerned with being culturally relevant, identifying with latest musical trends. If the contemporary Church can ever find its way back to seeking after God's presence and being sensitive to the Holy Spirit, we will find that when He begins to really show up, He will draw near all men to Himself.

We have crossed the line in too many congregations of marginalizing the Holy Spirit for the sake of attracting Man. And then once we get them within the four walls of the church we are ultra-careful not to offend them. But, if we could really make a resting place for the Lord and begin to minister to Him simply out a desire to minister to Him, we would find ourselves in the anointing of His Presence, rather than a contrived religious atmosphere. It's in His Presence where real freedom in found – a freedom that transcends cultural differences and traditional strategies.

In January 2000, I believe the Lord gave me a word of exhortation for many churches. I call it "A Season for New Songs". The following is the gist of it:

"The Lord says that a New Song is being released to His people. God is breathing a fresh wind of prophetic creativity on the artists and worship leaders. This wind will fill the sails of many congregations with a deeper understanding in their hearts of the goodness and the purposes of God for His people and the world at this time.

The Lord showed me a funnel of His light coming down from Heaven towards those who have been seeking His face and waiting on Him. The funnel was coming in a downward spiral. All who were underneath it and around it began to be caught up in a greater clarity of the light of His Presence. A great freedom came to many to lose themselves in the love and freedom of the Holy Spirit. But, as this funnel landed on many I could see musical notes like on a song sheet begin to blow back up the funnel towards Heaven.

The Lord says the Tabernacle of David is in the process of restoration. The Holy Spirit is releasing a hunger for the wisdom of worship that David and the Levites who ministered at David's tabernacle walked in. Many who have never had an appetite for extended periods of prayer and worship are going to begin having a burning heart for ministering to the Lord, as Mary did, with extravagant worship. They are going to learn to take the precious perfume of the passion of their hearts and waste it on Jesus' feet. But as they do this the perfume of the sweetness of Jesus' presence is going to begin to fill houses of worship in a deeper way. Many congregations are going to start spending what formerly would have seemed inordinate amounts of time singing, praying, dancing and just being in His presence.

In this fresh wind there is also going to be a great release of creativity. New songs are going to be stirred up in the hearts of artists and worship leaders. They will be prophetic in that they are going to help the Bride of Christ understand and perceive the heart, majesty, grace, and love of her lover – the King of kings. And just as leaders need like David to pay the price of building their own altars, the Lord says those leaders need to begin to make room in the sanctuaries for the people to minister to God. A shift is coming in these months and years we are now in. Many churches are no longer going to be centered solely on attracting man and ministering to man. The Father is pursuing those who will worship Him in Spirit and in Truth. He is pursuing those who desire to make a resting place, not merely a work place, for His Holy Spirit.

Just as David established a tabernacle of continuous worship, so many churches are going to also start establishing places continually open for prayer and meetings lasting all night in a desire to celebrate God and raising up a canopy of worship for God's Spirit to enjoy. And just as David's tabernacle had no veil, so in these places of worship the glory of God will be greatly known.

This is a time and season for the artists and worship leaders to enter into their priesthood in deeper dimensions. For the Lord says that if they shall be like Obed-Edom, who loved God's glory, they shall indeed, not just sing the songs and play the instruments, but they shall become Gatekeepers for many to help them move past the gates of thanksgiving and the courts of praise and into the glory of His Presence. They shall in fact, help the people build a resting place with a canopy of worship for His majesty.

It is time for the singers to sing a new song. It is time for the painters to paint with fresh colors. It is time for the dancers to dance as David did. It is time for the Levites to emerge and to offer up sacrifices of hearts burning for Him and the incense of true worship and prayer. It is time for the tent of His Glory to be re-established."

Several pastors who received this word favorably have asked me if I thought that God was saying each congregation was to begin to have 24/7 houses of prayer and worship established. My response has been categorically "No". What I do believe the Lord is attempting to say to the Church is "It's time to move into deeper intimacy with Me." Isaiah told a barren widow to,

"Enlarge the place of your tent, stretch your tent curtains wide, do not hold back, lengthen your cords, strengthen your stakes."   (Isaiah 54:2 NIV)

Each congregation, in each city should have its own unique ways of ministering to the Lord according to our God-given distinctives. The Lord never calls us to conformity in the way in which we reflect His Name and Love. But, He is calling all of us to open up the curtains of our hearts and give Him more ground in the Church. The promise is that if we will truly make a resting place for Him, the weary and broken will, in response, come and find rest in Him.

This is not to say we are not called to actively pursue evangelizing our streets and cities. But what it does mean is that if we will get the truly fresh bread back in the house, then the lost, the widows, the orphans, and all who are truly hungry and desperate will hear the Good News.

The noted thief, Willie Sutton, when asked why he robbed banks replied, "Because that's where the money is!" Why ascend "the hill of the Lord" if one is already "saved" and knows Jesus? Because that's where more of the Lord can be found.

"He who forms the mountains, creates the wind, and reveals His thoughts to man, he who turns dawn to darkness, and treads the high places of the earth – the LORD God Almighty is his name." (Amos 4:13 NIV)

Ascending the Hill of the Lord

There was a time before the fall of man, when God could be found walking in the cool of the day in the Garden. He was easily accessible and known. But when sin entered the picture He was forced to close off the Garden which is now fiercely protected by an angel with a fiery sword (Genesis 3:24). Even today as Christ has made the throne of God accessible again, we still find ourselves seeing "but a poor reflection as in a mirror". The time will come when *"we shall see face to face"* and know not just in part but fully (1 Corinthians 13:12). But what does one who has a "heart after God" do in the meantime? He or she must ascend the Hill of the Lord!

The Bible is filled with a many stories and pictures of God meeting with people in the high places. In very rare cases even in the third heaven as both Paul and Isaiah experienced – only accessible to us by a sovereign act by God. High places, naturally speaking, are accessible if one chooses to make the effort – the peaks of hills, the summits of mountains etc. Moses regularly ascended the hill in order to meet with God. Elijah climbed to the top of Mt Carmel and prayed for a drought to be broken. Jesus took Peter, James and John up the mount of Transfiguration where they beheld Him in His glory, along with Moses and Elijah. Jesus met the disciples supernaturally in Acts 2 in an upper room. Even Peter's revelation, as recorded in Acts 10, which led to the first Gentile converts happened while he was praying on a roof top!

To gain insight into what it means to "ascend the hill of the Lord" let's look at Moses' prayer and subsequent action in Exodus chapters 33 and 34. At this point in the saga of the

Hebrew's expedition from Egypt to a promised land flowing with milk and honey they are now approximately three months into their journey. They have experienced numerous signs and wonders from God, both before their release and since their departure from Egypt. They have had a miraculous deliverance and victory over Pharaoh's army by passing through the Red Sea on dry ground. God has given them water out of a dry rock and quail and bread from heaven. They have experienced a supernatural victory over the Amalekites when they were attacked at Rephidim.

However, after all of these great miracles and signs of God's faithfulness they turned to worshipping a false god and made a golden calf, even while Moses was on Mt Sinai communing with God on their behalf. In judgment, God caused a plague to break out amongst the people which killed many of them. The Lord relents though and continues to give Moses direction in order to bring the people into His great promises. Although God is merciful and gracious being willing to continue bearing with them, Moses is beginning to realize it is going to be a long and arduous road ahead trying to lead the people. So, in a place of personal desperation, he cries out for God to personally meet with him. You would think that already having experienced a great and unusual anointing of His Presence, complete with supernatural signs and wonders, supernatural provision and great breakthroughs against their enemies most, if not all pastors would be more than satisfied. Not Moses, however!

Moses was hungry for much more than anointing or success as a leader. He was a man of humility. He was a man who was desperate for God Himself. After God giving him such a powerful and wonderful promise he pressed in even more on God. *"Now show me your glory"*, he prayed (Exodus 33:18).

God's glory "passes by"

That prayer of Moses' is possibly one of the most audacious prayers found in the entire Bible. One can almost sense the wonder and trepidation of the angels as this mere mortal, a member of a fallen, sin-filled race, dares to ask God to show him His very being. But Moses was truly praying in his heart in line with the will of God. He had understood that what God really desired was to raise up a people who would, first and foremost, want Him. God had always envisioned humanity as a people to shower His love on and who in turn would reciprocate with a longing for Himself. And as daring a prayer as it was, it went straight to the heart of God. We are often like James and John who asked Jesus if they could be seated in heaven at His immediate side. He responded "You don't know what you are asking." Moses did have an idea of what he was asking for, but still he dared to press in on God.

God, because He is completely and utterly holy, cannot allow any sin whatsoever in His immediate presence otherwise, not only the sin, but the sinner would be consumed. And even though Moses was a man who walked in righteousness and humility, his righteousness was "as a filthy rag" in comparison to God. So God could not allow Moses to really see His face, but He could allow Moses to ascend the Hill of the Lord and stand on a rock and see His glory in passing. But as to His very being, He said,

> *"You cannot see my face, for no one may see me and live,"*
> (Exodus 33:20)

So the Lord directed Moses to,

> *"Be ready in the morning, and then come up on Mount Sinai. Present yourself to me there on top of the mountain."*
> (Exodus 34:2)

The next day, as instructed, Moses did ascend to the top of Mt Sinai. The Lord had provided a rock for Moses to stand on with a cleft, or cut, in it.

In David's eloquent Psalm 40 we read,

> *"I waited patiently for the Lord,*
> *he turned to me and heard my cry.*
> *He lifted me out of the slimy pit,*
> *out of the mud and mire;*

> *he set my feet on a rock*
> *and gave me a firm place to stand.*
> *He put a new song in my mouth,*
> *a hymn of praise to our God.*
> *Many will see and fear*
> *and put their trust in the LORD."*   (Psalm 40:1–3 NIV)

There is a rock that cannot be shaken. A foundation, which when built on, no winds of adversity can dislodge us from. And like the rock Moses stood on to gaze on God, this rock too has been cut. The name of this rock is Jesus of Nazareth – the Messiah. He was pierced through for our sins and when we stand in His mercy and grace there is a freedom to really know God, as opposed to merely knowing about Him.

This is the divine invitation of the cross. To go beyond the blessings, and seek the face of the *Blesser* Himself. Unlike Moses who approached God before the events of the cross, we can approach the very "throne of grace with confidence". Far too many settle for the blessings of the lowlands when the greatest treasure of all, His presence, is beckoning us to come to the High Places.

When Moses ascended the Hill of the Lord and stood on that chosen rock of God, he was allowed to see at least some of God's glory as it passed by. The Levitical Priests dared to approach the Holy of Holies, risking death and judgment, but found forgiveness and grace at the Mercy Seat, the resting place of God. In the same way, Moses too had a revelation of God's awesomeness, but also His great compassion. As Moses stood on the rock and called on the name of the Lord, God caused His glory to be visible as cloud and passed by Moses. As He did so, God proclaimed of Himself,

> *"The LORD, the LORD, the compassionate and gracious God, slow to anger, abounding in love and faithfulness, maintaining love to thousands, and forgiving wickedness, rebellion and sin."*   (Exodus 34:6–7a NIV)

When Moses dared to press deeper into the higher calling of seeking God's face, he came into a whole new revelation of God's heart – one of love, grace and mercy. The Israelite's when invited by God to draw near to Him and become a nation of priests, had grown afraid of the presence of God and run from the mountain of the Lord. The Bible says that when the people *"saw the thunder and lightning and heard the trumpet and saw the mountain in smoke, they trembled with fear. They stayed at a distance"* (Exodus 20:18 NIV).

But in this passage, perhaps the King James Version gives a more accurate rendering of the Hebrew word *nuwa* which the NIV translates as "stayed". The word implies to move, or to step down, to change position. The King James reads,

> *"And all the people saw the thunderings, and the lightnings, and the noise of the trumpet, and the mountain smoking: and when the people saw it, they removed, and stood afar off."*

The people had been given an invitation to be "a kingdom of priests", that is, a people who would draw near to God. But when the manifest presence of God came with thunder, lightning and smoke from the mountain as signs of God's power and majesty, the people *withdrew* out of fear – they *removed* themselves. While it is true that God was not allowing the people to come too close to Him, the parameters given them proved too much and they ran out of fear of His wrath. But, when one with a pure heart and clean hands dares to really draw near to God out the sole ambition of love for God, He always allows His heart to be more fully seen. To the pure God always shows Himself pure (Psalm 18:26) tells us. And according to Jesus,

> *"Blessed are the pure in heart, for they shall see God."*
>   (Matthew 5:8).

Lessons from mountain climbing

During most of the 1970s and the early 1980s, whilst in my late teens and early twenties, I did a lot of rock and mountain climbing. In fact, before God challenged me to give more of my time to ministry, some of the life goals I had were to attempt certain famous climbing routes. Those routes ranged from Yosemite Valley, in California, to the French Alps. Because I was not physically graced enough to be a really "natural" climber, I had to work and practice quite a bit to be a decent enough climber to do some of the routes which were only of average technical difficulty. Because it took a fair amount of my free time to maintain a standard, it began to interfere with time needed for prayer, personal Bible study and ministry. I was at a particular church meeting one night when I very clearly heard the Lord say to my heart that if I really wanted to go ahead with His call for my life, I was going to have to lay down climbing as it was beginning to be border on idolatry. What many of us fail to realize is that anything which can manipulate our hearts away from focusing on God is simply idolatry. That is not to say that in things like climbing, skiing, fishing, the arts, music etc., we can't enjoy the talents God has given us and the world which He has created. After all when God created the world and then Man in His image He saw that it was very good. However, the more fully we desire to walk in Christ's resurrection power, the more fully we need to embrace our own crosses!

Although, I never achieved the top standards of the day in rock climbing, I did climb and practice enough to learn some key lessons that applied not only to climbing, but to many areas of life, and especially, ascending the hill of the Lord. The first, and probably the most important was that true mountain climbing is not a "group event".

You can go to certain famous mountains, such as Mt Fuji in Japan, and there will be dozens of people at a time slowly hiking up the mountain. But that's not really technical climbing which requires both special equipment and training. Anyone, even a non-believer can attend a church meeting or conference and have a significant encounter with the Lord. But, most of the time those encounters are more an invitation to respond to the purposes of God. Just as when a first-time hiker in the mountains may be awestruck by the beauty of the mountains and decides to go on to make a serious decision to really try and become a mountain climber. But, once that person really gets into climbing he, or she, finds it is not a group activity when it comes to technical climbing. At the most, you will have three on a rope team, or sometimes two teams of two. Usually, however, it is two sharing a rope and sometimes even a solo activity.

It is one thing to attend a conference with several highly-anointed speakers and ministers. Especially if there are a couple of thousand people in attendance who all have faith to really experience the things of God. The Holy Spirit quite often responds to that high faith level and moves through the various anointings present. But what happens next week when the conference attendee goes home? What happens in the life of that person's own congregation? Are there really any changes in that individual's own walk with the God? Is that person now spending more time in prayer on their own, or does the conference merely become another spiritual snapshot they hang on their wall of experience, much like some people love to show pictures of their vacations?

Ascending the hill of the Lord is really only what you and I choose to do on a daily basis. It's as much a lifestyle as that of an experienced and successful mountain climber, or surfer. Many charismatic churches are filled with people who are conference junkies. Every couple of months they're off to the next great conference to hear the men and women with the hot messages. And they always have exciting reports of what God did during those conferences. But, unfortunately, the fruit of such meetings, other than some momentary excitement, never really becomes evident in their life or the life of their congregation, because they themselves never learn to ascend the Hill of the Lord on their own. Rather, they become what's known in climbing circles as an "armchair mountaineer" – someone who reads all the books about the great climbers, but never learns to do it themselves. Similarly, the contemporary Church must learn that revival is not an event that comes along like a train so that we can line up on the platform and jump aboard. Revival happens when enough Christians in one place begin to live biblical lives and seek God's face through prayer and worship, and reach out to the lost and hurting. When that begins to happen, we move from looking for revival, to *becoming the revival*. But true revival is not so much about corporate meetings, crowds and church growth as it is each of us *as individuals* daily meeting with God!

The second important lesson I learned from climbing is that the more difficult the mountain or route to ascend, the more preparation, work and determination is required. When I first began to become interested in mountain climbing I read a lot of books and especially some of the articles in *National Geographic*, that contained beautiful pictures of great majestic mountain faces, usually with a climber gracefully working their way up the route. What you find out when you begin to try and emulate what you see in the pictures however, is that it is *very hard work*. A technically difficult route can push you very quickly to the limits of your ability and strength. As you are concentrating with every bit of focus you have, with your feet on the smallest of footholds, stretching with one arm to a handhold high above you, meanwhile desperately trying not to lose your balance on a vertical rock face, your mind is screaming at you "What in the world are you doing here, your going to get yourself killed?!" Or perhaps, you're at high altitude on a 75 degree ice slope, huffing to keep some oxygen in your lungs, meanwhile trusting your body and sanity to two tiny protrusions sticking out of the front of your crampons, strapped to your boots, barely holding your weight onto the ice. The thought lurking in the back of your mind, somewhere between the conscious and the subconscious, is that if you ever get off this mountain you'll never do it again! Most of the routes one finds in guide books, from the Andes to the Alps, from the Sierra Nevada to the Himalayas, all require great determination and perseverance. As well, they quite often require quite a lot of work merely to arrive at the base of the mountain to begin the climb.

As it is in the natural, so it is in the spiritual realm. Our churches are filled with people who want to cruise in on a Sunday morning and get a blessing to last them through the week. They're far too busy throughout the week doing their thing to have any time for God. Before we are going to see a revival that will seriously touch our cities, we need to see a revival hit our hearts and local congregations in a serious way. We need men, women and children to rise up today, who are more concerned about getting hold of God than His quick fixes. When we can even come to a semblance of a reflection of how Jesus was, filled with the life and power of the Holy Spirit, we won't have to worry about coming up with slick programs to attract crowds. The desperate and the lost will respond like blind Bartimeus, as Jesus walked through Jericho. We won't be able to keep them away!

Lastly, a final lesson to consider is that the higher the mountain one climbs, the great the vision one has from the top. Admittedly, this is an obvious point. But the world and the Church is filled with people with great questions and insecurities concerning the future. Especially in the wake of the terrorism of September 11th, 2001. What's going to happen to the economy? Will my company ever downsize me? In the changing world of technology will my job skills become redundant? Even mature Christians still face constant questions concerning the next step in the road God has set before them. As one friend of mine puts it "God usually doesn't give maps, just compass settings". And while that's true, we all need from time to time a fresh sense of perspective and to see the lay of the land up ahead.

The Bible contains myriad wonderful promises concerning God's faithfulness in caring for us and watching over us. Those promises are to become our foundations in faith as we learn to get out of the boat of self-centeredness and control and begin to trust Him. The specifics however, as to the where's and when's in the journey of life are to come from the leading of the Holy Spirit. The Hebrews as they traveled through the wilderness were led by a pillar of fire by night and a cloud of glory by day. Jesus after coming out of the Jordan after being baptized by John, was led by the Holy Spirit into the desert for 40 days of communing with the Father. Why didn't He go straight into preaching, healing and deliverance instead? Because that wasn't how the Father wanted Him to begin. So, if Jesus was led by the Spirit, how much more dependent should we be on prayer and waiting on the Lord, rather than constantly running off to attempt our thing? Our churches in North America are constantly running from one program to the next, all promising to bring in a harvest. But, if Jesus only did the things He saw the

Father doing (John 5:19–20; 8:28–29), how much more should we realize the need for seeing and hearing what the Lord is wanting to show and say to us?

The great key to developing "eyes to see, and ears to hear" what the Holy Spirit is saying, is not seeking after a vision, but simply seeking after the One who gives vision. When we ascend the Hill of the Lord and spend what to some seems a waste of time – just ministering to Him – we begin to see things through His eyes. The dullness that obscures the eyes of our hearts becomes washed away by the balm of the Holy Spirit. We begin to realize God's greatest will for us is not really to do with where we are at and what we are doing, but rather *who we are* and where we are at *with Him*. One can constantly be wondering "What is the will of God for my life?" When we begin to fulfill the greatest commandment of loving Him with all of our hearts and become people who constantly worship Him, in the process the other questions and inner battles begin to fade away. All of a sudden prayer is not so much a chore but a privilege. All of a sudden evangelism becomes the fruit of a healthy vine firmly attached to the tree of life, Jesus. When we return to the simplicity of devotion to Christ Jesus and He begins to become the object of our focus, everything else begins to be seen with clarity. And as we begin to go from glory to glory, rather than trial to trial, we realize it's not so much what we know when questions and difficulties come along, but it's *Who* we know and *how well we know Him* that leads us into victory. When one is standing on the peak of a high mountain, not only is the view stupendous, but what was formerly hidden and out of view is now seen with ease. All of the labor, difficulty and cost involved, fade away as the heavens begin to open up. It's at this point that we know experientially the great promise of God recorded by Isaiah.

> *"Those who hope in the LORD will renew their strength. They will soar on wings like eagles; they will run and not grow weary, they will walk and not be faint."*
> (Isaiah 40:31 NIV)

Chapter 11

Pure Hearts and Clean Hands
(part 2)

In the previous chapter we looked a the motivating factor for desiring to ascend the Hill of the Lord. As we continue our study we read in Psalm 24 a rhetorical question posed by David.

> *"Who may ascend the hill of the LORD?*
> *Who may stand in his holy place?"*

The question before us is, who is qualified to actually make the ascent? As mentioned previously in connection with mountain climbing, without the proper preparation and determination, there were many climbs that were simply impossible to do, no matter how much you desired to do it. The same is true of ascending the Hill of the Lord. There are many people who, in public worship and prayer meetings, cry out "God, I just want more of you". That prayer is a wonderful prayer, and is a deep response of our hearts to the heart of God, prompted by the Holy Spirit within. However, too many people choose to disqualify themselves from the very thing they say they desire most.

The cost of ascending the Hill of the Lord is possessing "pure hearts and clean hands". We may believe completely in the Lord Jesus and His saving grace, and yet still not know the Lord intimately and be able to walk in His empowering grace, and to gaze on His beauty. You may be "saved", but are you a disciple of Christ? Do you know God only vaguely, or are you a *friend* of God? The friends of God usually have at least two things in common – clean hands and pure hearts.

We need to pass through both the Altar of Burnt Offerings and the Laver to achieve this. These Temple articles are symbolic of the need for our hearts to be purified by the consuming fire of God, and of our need for the "surface" cleansing of our various sins and bad attitudes. These are experiences that we have with God as He works in us by His Holy Spirit. Sadly, too often when contemporary preachers and Bible teachers speak on personal holiness they fall into the trap of legalism. Is God calling the Church today to walk in holiness? Absolutely! Can we, in and of ourselves, earn the love of God? Absolutely not! Holiness must be understood from a comprehensive biblical perspective, otherwise it brings condemnation and death rather than encouragement and life. On the other hand, it is equally dangerous to pursue the things and person of God without a clear understanding that the Lord God Jehovah is a completely Holy God who will not allow sin, or sinners for that matter, to abide in His presence.

So what exactly is the true holiness that God is after? God desires more than merely the absence of sin. The wages of sin are death, so an absence of sin is important, but what does that really look like as far as a lifestyle? God is so completely free of sin that it is impossible to live up to His standards. As Isaiah the prophet said (a man who had experienced the reality of God's holiness),

> *"All of us have become like one who is unclean, and all our righteous acts are like filthy rags."*   (Isaiah 64:6)

There is no one, no matter how holy we think we are, who walks in sinless perfection. And even when we are holy in our behavior in comparison with one another, the fruit, although good, is not the best. It is self-righteousness. What God is after is holiness of the heart!

The "practice" of sin

There is however, a major difference between occasionally committing minor sins and doing what the apostle Paul called "practicing" sin. To occasionally think a low or evil thought, to occasionally speak out of anger, jealously or selfishness, is a far cry from giving oneself license to commit definite sin as defined by the Bible over and over. Paul wrote to the church in Galatia,

> *"Now the deeds of the flesh are evident, which are: immorality, impurity, sensuality, idolatry, sorcery, enmities, strife, jealousy, outbursts of anger, disputes, dissentions, factions, envying, drunkenness, carousing, and things like these, of which I forewarn you just as I have forewarned you that those who practice such things shall not inherit the kingdom of God."*   (Galatians 5:19–21 NASB)

The word *practice* means "to do the same thing over and over until one begins to do that thing well". This is the biblical "line in the sand". I believe that it is critically dangerous for a Christian to cross over that line – to become a *practicer* of sin.

A Christian can fall and occasionally commit most sins without fear of losing their salvation. The apostle John when speaking on the subject said,

> *"If we confess our sins, he is faithful and just and will forgive us our sins and purify us from all unrighteousness."*
> (1 John 1:9 NIV)

However, and this is quite critical to understand, Christians as well as non-Christians can, and often do, reap what they sow when they commit sin. For example, a Christian businessman employed by a secular corporation may end up sinning by getting drunk at a company New Year's Eve party. He may never have become drunk before in his life but now, for the first time he does. Is it a sin to become drunk? Yes, the word of God is quite clear about drunkenness. Will God forgive him, or her, for becoming drunk? Yes, if they repent over it. But, what if on the way home from the party he, or she, is pulled over by the police for driving under the influence of alcohol? Or even worse, what if they accidentally kill someone due to driving under the influence? Will

God forgive them? Yes. But, they will still reap what they have sown. They will suffer the pain of grieving the Holy Spirit, the possible loss of reputation and what that may mean for the gospel in the eyes of his, or her, unsaved colleagues. And if they did go on to do someone grievous harm by drunken driving, the pain which the victim and their family suffer, as well as their own conscience, will continue for years to come. Will God forgive? Yes. Will they reap the consequences of their actions? Yes.

Two critical elements pertaining to sin must be understood. First, when a Christian gives room to sin in their life, they grieve the Holy Spirit on several levels. Firstly, even though God loves us all the time, when we entertain an evil thought or attitude, or when we go on to commit the sin, we quench and grieve the Holy Spirit. He is nothing less than *the Holy Spirit of the Living God*! And when we ignore Him and go on to do things contrary to the Word of God we offend Him, and to a degree, shut Him down, because He will not violate our own free wills.

Secondly, when we continue to give room to a sin on an ongoing basis we are giving access to demonic influence in our lives. Can a Christian become demonically possessed? No, not if he/she truly belongs to God. But can a Christian become demonically oppressed? Yes, if they give room through sin to the enemy. Sin is Satan's legal territory. When an individual, Christian or non-Christian, spends time in the enemy's territory, they come under the system of the law. For the non-Christian it's a matter of losing ever more of their life, cut off and separated from the fullness of God's love and protection. But for the Christian who sins it's a matter of belonging to one kingdom, a very good kingdom, and vacationing in an evil kingdom. The longer a Christian spends time in the enemy's camp, the more room and control they are surrendering to the enemy.

Consider for example, the parable Jesus told in Matthew 18 concerning the sin of holding onto unforgiveness.

> *"Therefore, the kingdom of heaven is like a king who wanted to settle accounts with his servants. As he began the settlement, a man who owed him ten thousand talents was*

brought to him. Since he was not able to pay, the master ordered that he and his wife and his children and all that he had be sold to repay the debt. The servant fell on his knees before him. 'Be patient with me,' he begged, 'and I will pay back everything.' The servant's master took pity on him, canceled the debt and let him go. But when that servant went out, he found one of his fellow servants who owed him a hundred denarii. He grabbed him and began to choke him. 'Pay back what you owe me!' he demanded. His fellow servant fell to his knees and begged him, 'Be patient with me, and I will pay you back.' But he refused. Instead, he went off and had the man thrown into prison until he could pay the debt. When the other servants saw what had happened, they were greatly distressed and went and told their master everything that had happened. Then the master called the servant in. 'You wicked servant,' he said, 'I canceled all that debt of yours because you begged me to. Shouldn't you have had mercy on your fellow servant just as I had on you?' In anger his master turned him over to the jailers to be tortured, until he should pay back all he owed. This is how my heavenly Father will treat each of you unless you forgive your brother from your heart.''

(Matthew 18:23–35 NIV)

The bottom line is found at the end of the parable when Jesus said that the servant who chose not to forgive the debts owed him would be, *"turned him over to the jailers to be tortured, until he should pay back all he owed. This is how my heavenly Father will treat each of you unless you forgive your brother from your heart."* Many Christians suffer a lack of peace, lack of joy and unnecessary strife in their souls. They can quote all the promises of the Bible, but still they fail to really experience many of those promises. The problem, much of the time, is that even though in general their sins are forgiven and they are bound for Heaven, there are still areas of their hearts that are dominated by things such as greed, lust, anger, unforgiveness, jealousy, etc., which have become like rooms in a hotel rented out to an evil guest. The overall building may be owned by God, but the supervisor of the building has given access through sin to the wrong sort of tenant. When we do that, there are areas of our hearts that suffer from torture from the jailer. We are under grace, but when we fail to surrender an area of our life to God, that area slips back under the law. And sin is Satan's legal territory.

When sin is left unchecked the heart can gradually become hardened. Slowly, over a prolonged period of sin, the Christian is slowly walking away from God. No one can take us out of Jesus' or the Father's hands (John 10:28–29). But, because we have free wills we can choose to walk away from His love and rule in our lives. Will one sin cause us to lose our salvation? No, not according to the apostle Paul. It must also be clearly understood that there is a difference between being tempted by the enemy and entertaining that temptation to the point where we give ourselves over to the sin. Even Jesus was tempted by Satan, but He never for a moment gave any place for the seeds of sin – temptation – to lodge in the soil of His soul and grow.

If we begin to practice sin we can slowly, over time, give so much room to the jailer and his henchmen, that we can no longer sense the Spirit of God, because in effect we have given ourselves over to the reign of the evil one. There are those who claim "once saved, always saved". I believe that to be true – to a point. There is a line we hopefully cross with God, where we have truly experienced so much of His goodness, love and grace, that we know in the depths of our hearts we never again can give ourselves over to sin. Are we perfect from that time on? No, but one is usually very quick to sense the grief he or she has caused the Holy Spirit, and that person tends to place a high value on living a lifestyle focused as much on repentance as blessing. In short, once one really becomes the friend of God there is such an ongoing and growing revelation of God's holiness, majesty and grace that you live and breath from a posture of humility and thanksgiving. Once one has truly stood in the light of the Truth Himself, you see sin as it truly is – ugly and cancerous!

The apostle Paul's letter to the Colossians warns us that if we have truly become reconciled to God *"by Christ's physical body through death to present you holy in his sight, without blemish and free from accusation"* we must *"continue in* [our] *faith, established and firm, not moved from the hope held out in the gospel.*" But, when one is closer to what some have called "carnal Christianity", there tends to be a dullness in the heart because of the continual grieving of the Holy Spirit. All too often that person ends up walking away from God. That person may also say "Christianity didn't work for me, I couldn't live up to the standards. I never experienced any peace, joy or self-control." The problem was that they might have gone forward at an altar call for salvation, but they never really got to know the person of Jesus. For many, Christianity never grows from the "free life insurance" stage into a real relationship of love and surrender! Too many never grow from the desire for Heaven to the desire for God!

Not all sin is forgivable. There is one sin Jesus spoke of that is unforgivable, and that is to blaspheme the Holy Spirit. In Mark 3:22, some teachers of the law said of Jesus, after He had cast out demons, *"He is possessed by Beelzebub! By the prince of demons he is driving out demons."* Several verses later, Jesus warned that they, the critical teachers, were in grave danger because they were speaking evil of the Spirit of God. He said in verses 28 and 29,

> *"I tell you the truth, all the sins and blasphemies of men will be forgiven them. But whoever blasphemes against the Holy Spirit will never be forgiven; he is guilty of an eternal sin."*

His statement was completely unequivocal – the accusation that the work being done by the Holy Spirit, through Jesus, was actually being done instead by a demonic power, was a most serious sin. Today there are many critics within the Body of Christ who are on very dangerous ground. It's too easy to make the mistakes of the Pharisees of Jesus' day. They automatically dismissed as demonic any experience they heard of which they themselves had not previously experienced. Obviously there is much happening in the world which is rooted in the demonic and witchcraft. But all too often, spiritual pride can rob us of objectivity and we think we have become the standard by which the Bible is measured.

The fire of God

The Bible often uses the picture of fire in association with the holiness of God, and with the cleansing process that He calls us to. Consider the judgement of Adam and Eve, following their rebellion against God, as recorded in Genesis 3.

> *"So the* Lord *God banished him from the Garden of Eden to work the ground from which he had been taken. After he drove the man out, he placed on the east side of the Garden of Eden cherubim and a flaming sword flashing back and forth to guard the way to the tree of life."*
>
> (Genesis 3:23–24 NIV)

A permanent barrier of fire was placed by the Lord to keep Man from coming back into His immediate presence. That fire was actually a sword wielded by a cherubim, one of the type of angels who are continuously in God's very presence. Similarly, any time Man seeks to resume a relationship of intimacy with God, the consuming fire of His presence must be embraced. Moses, after a forty year time of preparation in the wilderness, ascended the hill and gazed on the bush of fire. Isaiah, when brought up to the throne room of God, needed to be touched on the lips by a piece of flaming coal – representing the fire of God's presence. It is of great interest that, although Isaiah could be touched by burning coal, the angel could only touch it with tongs:

> *"Then one of the seraphs flew to me with a live coal in his hand, which he had taken with tongs from the altar. With it he touched my mouth and said, 'See, this has touched your lips; your guilt is taken away and your sin atoned for.'"*
>
> (Isaiah 6:6–7 NIV)

Although the angels of God are more wise and powerful than we and completely sin-free, we, humanity, made in God's image, can be filled with the Spirit of God. Man alone, of all the creatures made by God, are the ones who by the blood of the Lamb, can actually be called "sons of God".

When I first came to the Lord Jesus through the Jesus movement in Southern California, I personally knew many young people who were zealously serving God. We were going out on the streets doing evangelism and trying every way we could to serve God. But today, some 25 years later, many of those friends are no longer actively serving God, In fact, most of them are not even walking with God today. Many of their marriages have ended up in divorce and more than a few committed adultery leading to their divorces. How is it that when they were so on fire for God their flames could burn out? In retrospect we were excited about the promises and blessings of God. We were excited about Heaven to come. But, what we were not encouraged to do was to seek the face of God. We did repent of our obvious sins (the surface cleansing of the Laver), but we never embraced a deep, life-changing repentance (the deep cleansing of the Altar of Burnt Offering) and gave ourselves wholeheartedly to Him.

In a *Focus on the Family* magazine about a year ago, there was a short article by Scott Denicola. In that article he quoted statistics on divorce provided by Dave Kinnamon of Barna Research. According to Barna Research,

> "27 percent of Christian adults have gone through a divorce, compared to 21 percent of atheists. The national average (of marriages which end in divorce) is 25 percent."

These are astounding figures when you consider the fact that Christians are people who claim to be living by God's standards of love, humility and commitment. How is this possible? I believe the answer is quite simple. We have been trying to live up to God's holy standards without allowing our hearts to be cleansed by a personal passion for Him. We have tenaciously clung to His promises and blessings, but have neglected the great commandment of first loving God with all of our hearts. Christian counselors are busy trying to dress the wounds of the sheep, but until the *hearts* of the sheep become healed, they will continue to wander into thorny and rocky soil which brings hurt and ruin to the soul.

And because Christians are more aware of God's standards than the world, they find it even harder to live with the knowledge of their guilt.

As Paul stated in Romans 4:15, the *"law brings wrath. And where there is no law there is no transgression."* When someone outside the family of God, ignorant of God's higher standards, commits sin, they are not always aware of it because of their hardened hearts. Christians who are living in troubled or abusive marriages are very, very aware of falling short of God's standards, whereas their non-Christian neighbors may be unaware of any higher standard which surpasses their experience. And if they are not in a tight relationship with God, they are unable to draw from God's heart and Spirit, the love, power and humility necessary to repair the marriage. Subsequently they often cannot go on living with the guilt and tension hanging over them. Meanwhile, their neighbors, who will be answerable to God on day of judgement, don't know any better. They, unlike their Christian neighbor, may be willing to muddle on with a shaky marriage.

It is the fire of God which not only takes away sin and guilt, but much more importantly, cleanses our hearts of the very weakness that makes us vulnerable to temptation. Superficially clean hands are not enough! If we really want to see the Lord we must allow Him to purify our hearts!

Chapter 12

The Money Issue

You may ask, "What has money got to do with our seeing more of God in our cities and nations?" Actually, it has everything to do with it. How we handle money, more than any other item in our life, indicates where our hearts are truly at. For this reason Jesus taught more parables concerning the proper use of money than on any other topic.

In many church circles there is a false dichotomy between what is considered spiritual and what is considered earthly, or non-spiritual. However, the Bible tells us that every good and perfect gift comes from God, the Father of light. Everything in our lives, except sin of course, is good and has value if properly stewarded. Many churches that have entertained an unbiblical theology of separation between the spiritual and the physical, have also fallen prey to what can be called a spirit of poverty. Because they do not understand God's care, provision and involvement in the basic needs of this life they tend to be clinging and grasping with their financial resources. And rather than being free to fully enjoy all of God's blessings they end up like the rich miser who not only never shares what he has, but is also unable to enjoy it himself. Christians who are not really able to be gracious with the tools of this realm, are invariably not entrusted by God with the more precious gifts of the Holy Spirit!

The sin that Malachi identifies in Malachi 3 is a basic mistake that a lot of Christians make today. Out of mistrust and misunderstanding of God's love and provision they tend to horde their finances, or at least spend selfishly, without recognizing that it all belongs to God! For those that have come to Christ Jesus everything in their lives is spiritual in the sense that every good and perfect gift come from God. And because we are bought with a price everything we possess belongs to God. Our jobs, our abilities and opportunities to make money, the inheritances which our earthly fathers give to us, all are orchestrated by God. In the handling of the finances and resources which come into our hands, we need to constantly remind ourselves that we are, in actuality, stewards rather than owners of these resources.

God does give us great leeway in the stewarding of what He entrusts us with. The difference between a steward and a slave, is that a steward supposedly is a person of wisdom and experience who can act on his, or her, master's behalf with discretion and wisdom, so that the master's wealth (or kingdom) might increase. Whereas a slave, is merely one who has to be watched over and given very implicit, basic instructions. A steward for a wealthy person tends to be much more on the level of an associate than merely a servant, slave or employee.

While God does give us latitude in administrating His resources, He also at times allows our hearts to be tested. Acts chapter 5 tells the story of a couple named Ananias and Sapphira who sold a piece of property. They proceeded to give *part* of the money of the sale to the Church. They then told the apostles that they had given *all the money of the sale*, rather than a portion of it, to the Church. The lie resulted in both their lives being taken by God. The sin of Ananias and Sapphira was not that they did not give *all* of the proceeds of the sale of their property to the Church, but rather that they lied about the amount of the sale (Acts 5:1–10) For example, it would not have been wrong, for Ananias and Sapphira to have saved part of it for their old age, or their children's inheritance. The latter is certainly biblical and the former is not unbiblical. God cared about their needs being met. The property and the proceeds from the sale were theirs to manage. Peter's words to Ananias were,

> *"Didn't it belong to you before it was sold? And after it was sold, wasn't the money at your disposal? What made you*

think of doing such a thing? You have not lied to men but to God."

Their sin was lying to God, not the improper use of money. Prior to the lie being told they were to be commended if anything, for giving away a good portion of the money, way beyond the tithe, to the Church.

God loves a party!

Many who tithe or give offerings, do so begrudgingly out of a sense of guilt and obligation. Guilt because, in not understanding the principle of tithing, their hearts are not in it. And out of obligation because, after all, the pastors need something to live on! While most can see that tithing does help meet the practical needs of the local congregation and its leaders, the biggest reason God has ordained tithing is a great surprise for many.

In Deuteronomy chapter 14 we read the following,

> *"Be sure to set aside a tenth of all that your fields produce each year. Eat the tithe of your grain, new wine and oil, and the firstborn of your herds and flocks in the presence of the LORD your God at the place he will choose as a dwelling for his Name, so that you may learn to revere the LORD your God always. But if that place is too distant and you have been blessed by the LORD your God and cannot carry your tithe (because the place where the LORD will choose to put his Name is so far away), then exchange your tithe for silver, and take the silver with you and go to the place the LORD your God will choose. Use the silver to buy whatever you like: cattle, sheep, wine or other fermented drink, or anything you wish. Then you and your household shall eat there in the presence of the LORD your God and rejoice."*
> (Deuteronomy 14:22–26 NIV)

So what is this actually saying? Let's make four simple observations that help to understand tithing from God's perspective. Firstly, we are to tithe, or give ten percent of everything we have that is income to the Lord. It all belongs to Him anyway, and every good gift comes from Him. Even though we may be laboring for that produce, it is still God that blesses us with the gifting, talents, ability, and opportunity to make that income. Secondly, giving the tithe was never intended by God to be burdensome. If the place of giving the tithe was simply too far away, then the Israelites were instructed to sell their produce (which is not a consideration for most today) for cash. Thirdly, and very importantly, when giving the tithe the Israelites were expected to celebrate. They were expected to eat, drink and celebrate the goodness of God in their lives. Moses instructed the Israelites that if the place was too far to take their cash and buy cattle, sheep, wine or other fermented drink, or anything they wanted and to eat in the Lord's presence and rejoice. This picture of a party going on during a time of tithing is certainly a far cry from most offering times in churches today, which usually resemble a funeral service rather than any sort of celebration!

Many of us, if we were to unexpectedly win a contest, or receive an inheritance worth millions of dollars would throw a party for our friends and neighbors to celebrate our good fortune. That sort of celebration presents a truer picture of what God intended our times of giving tithes and offerings to be like. When we tithe and give offerings it should never be simply out of duty, or necessity, but out of the joy of knowing that the living God has adopted us and is taking responsibility for our needs!

Lastly, and perhaps, most important of all, the giving of the tithe is holy to the Lord. We often refer to communion as "holy communion" because we understand the symbolism involved in "eating of Jesus' body" and "drinking His blood". But, God said that when the people were to give the tithe, and eat, drink and celebrate, they would be doing so in God's Presence. Of course, we understand that they were probably not experiencing a revelation of God's glory quite like Moses would when ascending the mountain of the Lord. Nonetheless, the promise of God was that when people did render back to God His tithe that God, who is Holy, would meet with them. And any event that involves the very presence of God is made holy by the fact of His presence.

In short, the giving of the tithe was never intended to be an obligatory, dry, religious act of burden. Rather it was intended by God to be a time of partying in God's midst while celebrating His goodness to us. I remember a few years ago when I was helping to lead a meeting at the Rock City Church pastored by Bart Pierce. Bart had asked me to take the offering. Their main worship leader at the time, happened to be a very gifted and anointed saxophone player. I felt we should take the offering as the worship leader played the saxophone in worship to the Lord, near where the ushers stood in the front of the sanctuary. I encouraged the people to give as they felt led in response to the goodness of God. As we began to worship God with our singing and our offerings a great sense of celebration fell on the place. Many people ended up running down to the front in order to put in their offerings. I was standing in the front row with Bart and I remember a man standing right behind me, rather aggressively moving forward and literally opening up his wallet and dumping in all the cash he had. Then whilst singing he returned to his seat. A moment later, he came forward a second time and threw in his whole wallet with all of his credit cards and everything else and returned to his seat singing again! Seconds later, he came forward a third time with his wife's purse and emptied out all her cash and change! Of course later on the wallet and credit cards were returned to the man, but in that "meeting place with God" he was doing something which was symbolically powerful. He was demonstrating in the midst of worship, that everything he had belonged to God, and he was beside himself with joy as he did so! We went on that night to have a profound time of worship. Truly where the Spirit is there is both liberty and liberality. Liberty to receive from God and liberality to give to God and one another!

Our problem is that too often we really fail to understand God the Father's heart and care for us, His children. When we come into relationship with the Father He does not give us the spirit of a slave, or an orphan. He gives the Spirit (His Holy Spirit) of Adoption (Romans 8:15) by which we become full heirs in the family of God. God becomes our *Jehovah Jireh* – the Lord God our Provider. This is the God whom the apostle Paul said would, *"meet all your needs according to his glorious riches in Christ Jesus"* (Philippians 4:19 NIV). The act of tithing is a celebration which helps us to remember God's incredible love, care and provision. It symbolizes the fact that our lives and everything else we have belongs to Him, and for that reason we have cause for celebration.

I have been with churches in Africa, for example, where they celebrate the opportunity to tithe by dancing to the front of the church while worshipping and put their tithes and offerings into a jar, or basket. What a far cry from most church services in the west churches where many pastors are almost embarrassed to take up the Sunday morning offering!

The point Malachi was making was that if we cannot trust God for our simple physical needs enough to be able to give back a symbolic ten percent of what belongs to Him anyway, than how, and why, should God ever trust us with the true wealth that He has to offer us. Not the fading riches of this realm that moth and rust can destroy, but the fellowship, revelation, anointing, peace, and joy that flows from His precious Spirit. Many Christians are like little children who have a great inheritance, but are not allowed control of it because of lacking basic maturity! Only a foolish parent would entrust the keys of a car to a teenager who can't even be trusted with taking out the trash. Those who have proven faithful with a little can then be trusted with more. But, those who have proven unfaithful with a little, sometimes, even what they do have is taken away!

Moses continued his instructions on tithing in Deuteronomy 14:27 by focusing the practical use of the tithe:

> *"And do not neglect the Levites living in your towns, for they have no allotment or inheritance of their own."* (NIV)

We are all called to serve God and Man out of God's love for us. There are those "living in our towns" (churches, communities etc.) – apostles, prophets, evangelists, pastors and teachers – that God has called into full-time ministry. They and their families have the same costs of living as everyone else in the Body of Christ. So tithing also becomes a provision which the Lord uses to meet the practical needs of His "priests", just as it did the Old Testament Priests who ministered in His temple.

I have heard the argument made that tithing is not for New Testament times. That it is simply an Old Testament carry over from the days when they had Levitical Priests. Of course, in New Testament thinking we are all called to be a nation of priests who minister to the Person of God, through prayer and worship. But, we still have those today that God calls to be separated into ministry. Speaking of the financial needs of those called to serve the church full-time, Paul wrote the following in his first letter to Timothy,

> *"The elders who direct the affairs of the church well are worthy of double honor, especially those whose work is preaching and teaching. For the Scripture says, 'Do not muzzle the ox while it is treading out the grain,' and 'The worker deserves his wages.'"*   (1 Timothy 5:17–18 NIV)

The term "double honor" here is especially referring to money in this context!

I have been deeply embarrassed for some churches I have ministered in, doing conferences and meetings, by the way the church failed to care financially for their pastor, or pastoral team. When God delegates authority and gifting to a leader, that leader has authority to care for that local church. When a church fails to take good financial care of their leader, in effect they are snubbing their noses at God's gift to them. Paul's words to Timothy were that these "gifts" were to be treated with double honor. When a minister, or church leader, is forced to live well below the level of the members of his congregation, that particular gift from God is being despised! And when a church despises the gifts of this realm, for sure God will not entrust that church with the gifts of the heavenly realms which really have worth!

We know from the way in which Jesus responded to the tempting of Satan in the wilderness that we are not to put God to the test. But, the exception to that rule is found in Malachi's rebuke over the people's failure to tithe. Malachi 3:10 reads,

" 'Bring the whole tithe into the storehouse, that there may be food in my house. Test me in this,' says the LORD Almighty, 'and see if I will not throw open the floodgates of heaven and pour out so much blessing that you will not have room enough for it.' " (NIV)

Malachi actually tells us to put God to the test when it comes to tithing. The reason so many Christians and churches fail to really grow into the blessings God has for them, is they simply don't believe in God's goodness enough to celebrate Him by tithing. And because of that many leaders end up having to continually fight feelings of inadequacy as their families are ill-cared for and their churches suffer from poor provision.

Overcoming the spirit of poverty

Among the various definitions that Merriam-Webster's Collegiate Dictionary offers of the word "poverty" there are two that are unfortunately, extremely relevant to many western congregations. The first is "the state of one who lacks a usual or socially acceptable amount of money or material possessions". The second is "a range from extreme want of necessities to an absence of material comforts". While most churches in western nations usually have some sort of building to meet in, unlike poor congregations in other parts of the world, too many churches, regardless of the size and beauty of the four walls they meet in, are living in a spiritual famine. Despite the preaching and teaching, there is too often a lack of peace, joy, and victory in the lives of the believers. Too many churches are missing the power and sense of awe that accompanies the presence of the Lord. The truth is, because God has found many congregations unable to trust Him with their tithes and offerings, He in turn, is unable to entrust them with the true wealth of the Holy Spirit which He so desires to give them!

Why is that when it comes to giving to God, who has given us His best – Jesus – the people of God are often severely lacking in resources? Many people have ingrained in their religious minds the view that money is earthly and therefore unimportant when it comes to the things of God. Why is that most Christians who hold to that view often fail to hold that same standard to their own lives? And for those who do embrace what I call a spirit (or mindset) of poverty, the question needs to be asked, "Is their religious view of money really biblical?" The answer, in general, is a resounding "NO".

If at this point, the previous paragraph is causing you to do emotional back flips I ask that you read on the next few pages. Let me begin by asking the reader not to respond with an intellectual knee-jerk reaction and assume I saying something I am not. I am not an advocate of Christians using biblical principles in areas such as prayer and giving as a means of becoming wealthy. Unfortunately, there are many Bible teachers and preachers who have allowed the value system of the world to permeate their theology to the point where God is simply a means of obtaining the riches of this world. Furthermore, there have been countless saints, not only in the history of the Church, but also today, that God has and does call to forsake much of the creature comforts of this world in order to minister exclusively to the poor, or for a life set apart for prayer and fasting.

However, unless such a vow of poverty comes from the leading of the Holy Spirit, it is simply a religious practice falsely replacing the will of God for a person's life. When Jesus said to the rich young man, *"Go, sell everything you have and give to the poor"*, He was speaking to one individual, not teaching the multitude. Whilst using prayer and faith as a means of gaining wealth is wrong, so on the other side of the pendulum, is trying to make a teaching or general principle out of a specific *rhema* word given to one person concerning a vow of poverty. It is not the money itself which is the root of all evil, but rather the love of it.

In general, when we read the whole Bible and what it has to say about God's provision we are constantly reminded of God's good care and provision to His children. Many confuse the lusting after materialism that our culture encourages with having our basic needs met. We can enjoy the wonderful provision of *Jehovah Jireh* – the Lord God our Provider.

Read for example Philippians 4:19:

"And my God will meet all your needs according to his glorious riches in Christ Jesus."

and Proverbs 22:4:

*"Humility and the fear of the LORD
bring wealth and honor and life."*

What wonderful examples of God's faithfulness! It is true that too many Christians are in bondage to Madison Avenue's dictates of success, but that cannot be allowed to detract from the fact that God is a good provider. Jesus, Himself, said that our heavenly Father is aware of our needs even before we ask. And in teaching the disciples a basic framework of how to approach the Father in prayer, He encouraged us to seek after Him for our daily needs.

When we look biblically at the full picture of God, we see that God is rich in glory, rich in resource, and rich in generosity. Without saying that wealth should be our standard, neither can we say that wealth is sin – otherwise we would have to find fault with God for blessing King Solomon with exceedingly great riches. Our problem some-times is we that fail to really appreciate the second point of the prayer Jesus taught the disciples:

"Thy Kingdom come [your reign, will, and provision] *on earth* [our situation] *as it is in Heaven."*

Psalm 34 is a wonderful song of worship by David which celebrates the Lord's love and care. In verse 9 he sings, *"Those who fear Him* [the Lord] *lack nothing."* In verse 10 he continues with the thought, *"Those who seek the Lord lack no good thing."* So our question might be, "What is a 'good thing' in the eyes of the Lord?" For many a family vacation at a place where the family can ski together for a week, or go sailing together, might seem rather frivolous and luxurious. But, for many families who can afford to do so, a week together at the beach, or in the mountains can be an incredible time of growing together and establishing essential bonds. Throughout the 1980s my wife and I went six years without taking a real vacation. This was partially due to not always having enough money for a time of really getting away, but was also partially due to having a spirit of poverty. I did not believe in God's love and provision enough to actually believe God would place any value on simply blessing my wife and me to get away and really relax together in a pleasant and stress-free setting. When we broke out of that cycle, my wife and I, and later with our young children, found those times of getting away and simply enjoying one another in a enjoyable and restful place, incredibly enriching as a family. There are seasons where God sometimes teaches us to be content with a little, or a lot, but often times the reason that we "don't have" is simply that we "don't ask"! And too often we do not ask because we have a false view of God being religious and miserly!

Again, there will no doubt be many who will ask themselves, "What is this chapter on money doing in a book about God and the increase of His kingdom?" However money, properly understood, must be included along with all the other resources that God entrusts to us: relationships, spiritual gifts and talents. He expects a return on all His investments, and money is not excluded! And because money is the measure of wealth and power in this realm, more than any other practical tool, He uses it as a yardstick to measure where our hearts are at. If we are grasping, greedy and covetous, denying Him His tithes and offerings when He prompts us to give, then He knows He cannot trust us with more of His Spirit and the gifts belonging to the Holy Spirit. Because as precious as the gifts of this realm are, the gifts of the Spirit are simply priceless. But, if we can prove to be generous, trusting and gracious with the perishable resources of this realm, God in turn can trust us to be generous, trusting, and gracious with the imperishable gifts which are eternal.

When a congregation has a good percentage of people that are merciful, gracious and giving out their love and security in Christ, God will pour out the rains of Heaven on them. The process starts first of all with us trusting God and His goodness who then, in turn, opens up the windows as we celebrate and give back to Him. Until that time, the windows will be firmly shut and we will not experience God's open heavens

The way out of the trap of poverty is to do the very thing that common sense and the value system of the world so strongly react against – to give, not horde! God longs for the Church to break out of the consumer orientated, self-centered mindset of the world and become like Him – givers rather than takers. To invest in love and relationships and learn to reap the harvest of faithfulness.

> *"Well done, good and faithful servant! You have been faithful with a few things; I will put you in charge of many things. Come and share your master's happiness!"*
>
> (Matthew 25:21 NIV)

Chapter 13

The Jacob Generation

God uses the "imperfect"

Because God's thoughts and ways are higher than Man's (Isaiah 55:9), God is often, to our limited minds, a God of paradoxes. For example, because He is completely holy, He cannot allow sinners to abide in His Presence, yet He loves sinners and reaches out to them with His whole heart. In fact, not only does He love sinners, but He delights in choosing very imperfect people to pour out His mercy and grace on. Often, not only does He choose such individuals who, to our minds we would readily reject as recipients of His love, but He shines a spotlight on them and uses them to bring glory to His Name in ways beyond our understanding.

One of the greatest examples in the New Testament is the apostle Paul, formerly known as Saul. Saul was one of the chief antagonists of the early Church. It was at his feet that the witnesses of Stephen's martyrdom laid down their garments. In other words, Saul more or less officiated the murder of Stephen (Acts 7:58). Acts 8:3 tells us that immediately following the stoning of Stephen, Saul *"began to destroy the church. Going from house to house, he dragged off men and women and put them in prison."* What a testimony! He was attempting to destroy the Church! That puts him in the same category as Nero, or others who have attempted to crush Christianity. In fact, Saul was traveling to Antioch for the purpose of having Christians arrested, locked up, and

tortured, when he was apprehended by the Holy Spirit. Yet
this is the very same man, renamed Paul, that the book of
Acts tells us took the gospel to the nations! He ended up
being one of the most influential of all the disciples,
performed powerful healings and miracles, wrote over half
of the New Testament, and was martyred for Christ!

Just as much of a paradox as God using Paul to shake the
world, was God's heart for Jacob thousands of years ago and
His heart for a *Jacob generation* today. After stating that God
would require clean hands and a pure heart of anyone who
would ascend the Hill of the Lord, David continued to say
that,

> *"He will receive blessing from the LORD*
> *and vindication from God his Savior.*
> *Such is the generation of those who seek him,*
> *who seek your face, O God of Jacob."*
>
> (Psalm 24:5–6 NIV)

God's choice in choosing Jacob over his brother Esau is more
than a little perplexing to the rational mind. Again, it
illustrates God's heart for those who have a heart after Him,
despite their shortcomings. Let's take a brief look at Jacob
and see what his experiences portend for our generations
today.

The very name Jacob means "supplanter" in the Hebrew
language. Jacob was actually the second born twin of Isaac,
one of the great patriarchs of the Hebrew people. Genesis
25:26 explains the reason for Jacob's name right at the point
of birth. As Esau came first out of his mother's womb, his
brother Jacob came out with his hand grasping Esau's heel.
So, he was named "Jacob". The word "tripper" as his birth
illustrates, is appropriately synonymous with the word
"supplanter". Later on in Genesis we see that Jacob was also
a liar. The predominant characteristic of Jacob's early years
as a young man, was that of seeking to supplant, usurp, and
trip up his brother, so that he did not receive his rightful
birthright as the eldest son. And what is shocking in the story
of Jacob, is the fact that God actually favored and rewarded
Jacob over his elder brother.

"When Isaac was old and his eyes were so weak that he could no longer see, he called for Esau his older son and said to him, 'My son.' 'Here I am,' he answered. Isaac said, 'I am now an old man and don't know the day of my death. Now then, get your weapons – your quiver and bow – and go out to the open country to hunt some wild game for me. Prepare me the kind of tasty food I like and bring it to me to eat, so that I may give you my blessing before I die.''

(Genesis 27:1–4 NIV)

In our western culture it may seem rather innocuous and quaint for Esau to want his father's blessing before he died. In the Middle Eastern culture of the Bible however, what this meant was the father's possessions and authority were passed on to the eldest son. In fact, it actually meant much more than this to the Hebrew people who were in a covenant relationship with God (Genesis 9:9). It meant much more than the blessing of man, or mere materialism. It meant to become *the* recipient of God's blessing of authority over your family. It was worth far more than silver or gold.

Esau was a strong and skilled hunter, so his father requested of him to go and kill some wild game and cook it for him. The insinuation from the continuing story is that Jacob lacked both his brother's strength and his hunting skills. In short, Jacob, by comparison, appears to be somewhat of a stay-at-home weakling, protected by his mother. Not the sort of man his father wanted to leave in charge of his name, fortune and the destiny of his family.

Under his mother's direction however, Jacob managed to convincingly lie to his father that he was Esau and returned home with the cooked game. In reality, he was serving him lamb cooked by his mother. Although his father recognized the voice of Jacob, because he was blind he was fooled by the smell of Esau's clothes which Jacob had put on. Jacob was also wearing some lambskin on his hands and arms to simulate his brother's more hairy skin. The deception worked. After eating the food prepared by Jacob's mother, Isaac gave his patriarchal blessing to Jacob, the second-born, who had fooled him.

When Esau returned with the game his father had requested, he was filled with wrath at Jacob for stealing his blessing. Jacob ended up running for his life out of fear of his brother's vengeance.

The question that rightfully comes to our minds is "What's the big deal? Even if you can fool a blind man out of a blessing, you can't fool God who sees everything. God would surely not honor a blessing stolen in deception, wouldn't He?" The truth that is God did honor the blessing given to Jacob precisely because *He did see* everything, including Jacob's and Esau's hearts. Even though Jacob was a liar, a schemer, a cheat and a thief, God saw beyond all of the outer flaws and looked upon his heart. His elder brother, who by law should have received the blessing from God, actually despised his spiritual inheritance in his heart. Genesis 25:29–32 tells us that Esau actually sold Jacob his birthright for the price of a cup of stew, merely because he was hungry! In God's heart there are some things worth far more than money, possessions or food. What is this factor that that has allowed some Christians to deny the Lord Jesus Christ at the threat of torture or death, while others did *"not love their lives so much as to shrink from death"*? It is the lack of heart-revelation of a love that is better than life itself.

I remember visiting a seminary class with a friend who was a student at Talbot Theological Seminary in the late 1970s. He had mentioned that the professor had promised a special guest for the class that afternoon who was not to be missed. As we waited wondering who was actually coming, in walked Corrie Ten Boom. She did not so much teach us, but rather in a quiet and humble way, told us simple stories from her decades of experience walking with God. One of those stories I will never forget. It was during World War II in Europe and she was part of a small prayer group in a German-occupied country, where it was forbidden by the Germans for the Christians to meet. One night, in the midst of their weekly meeting, there came a loud bang at the door and a German voice demanded that the door be opened. Their worst fears had been realized. They had been found out. In walked an officer of the greatly feared Gestapo with some soldiers. The soldier pointed their guns at the group while the officer calmly and quietly stared at them. She related to us how intimidating that stare had been. After a moment of silence the officer then said that if there were any present who did not really believe that Jesus Christ was Lord and Savior they were free to leave, or face the consequences. Much to the surprise of the overall group, a few of the Christians got up and left. Like Esau, selling his spiritual birthright, they preferred life in this realm than their promises in Christ.

The officer then commanded the soldiers to escort those who denied Jesus out of the building and to stand guard over them down in the street. The officer still stood silently and grimly surveying the remaining group as the stomp of the booted soldiers echoed down the stairs. If anything they were even more intimidated by the sole presence of the Gestapo officer than when he was accompanied by the soldiers. The reputation of the Gestapo was both vicious and horrible.

When all was completely quiet, the officer removed his hat and smiled, and to the great surprise of the Christians stated, "I too am a Christian and I want to worship with you. But, like you, I have to do it secretly and I could not risk betrayal by lukewarm Christians, so I was forced to test their commitment to Christ." They went on to have a wonderful time of worship and praying for each other with a great sense of the mercy and goodness of Christ!

Jacob was, beyond a shadow of a doubt, a sinner. He lied, he cheated and was a man without scruples. Yet, deep within his heart there was a profound longing for God and His love. And that was what God responded to. As God said to Samuel, "Man looks at the outward appearance, but I always look at the heart."

While Jacob was fleeing from the wrath of his brother, Genesis 28 tells us of an encounter that Jacob has with the presence of God. It was a sovereign act of God. The Lord decided that He needed to apprehend him, in order to begin to bring him in line with His purposes. There is pastor in Guatemala, who for many years now has been used powerfully to turn his community upside down for Christ. At one point in his life he was lying drunk on the floor of a bar, without any understanding of God. He then, like Jacob, began to experience a sovereign meeting with God. This drunken, hopeless, miscreant heard the voice of the Lord ask him, "Will you preach for Me?" What great Bible teacher or theologian would dare to point out a drunk in a bar, or an infamous persecutor of the Church like Paul, and see a future apostle or a preacher of the Gospel? We, with our finite understandings and perspectives usually cannot. But, God can, and often does, precisely because He is the Great I AM.

We are used to trying "religiously" to work things out for God in our feeble attempts to overcome the difficulties before us. We've somehow lost the lesson the apostle John modeled for us when he simply rested his head on Jesus' shoulder during a time of just relaxing in God's presence. Why did John turn out to be the most prophetic of all the disciples? The answer is found in seeing where the desire of his heart lay – to just be the friend of God. Or what about the young servant of Eli the priest, Samuel? At a time when the voice of God was absent from Israel he used to "sleep by the altar". We need a people today, who despite their questions and problems, will spend time laying their heads on the rock Himself, Jesus, rather than trusting in their own knowledge and understanding!

Jacob, in a place of fear and great unrest because he was fleeing from his angry brother, also laid his head on a rock and fell asleep. As he slept he received a wonderful prophetic dream from God concerning his future. He woke up however, realizing that he had experienced far more than a prophetic dream. He realized he had actually been in the awesome presence of the great I AM. He proclaimed,

> *" 'Surely the* LORD *is in this place, and I was not aware of it.' He was afraid and said, 'How awesome is this place! This is none other than the house of God; this is the gate of heaven.' "*   (Genesis 28:16–17 NIV)

Usually when preachers speak on this passage from Genesis, they focus on the dream, which we commonly refer to as Jacob's ladder. The dream did have great import for Jacob, and indeed, is relevant to the Church today. But the really significant thing that happened was not that God gave Jacob a wonderful dream and insight into his future, but He –

the Living God – came to that place and met with Jacob. That meeting profoundly changed Jacob's life and made him able to walk in the fulfillment of the dream.

We are so often focused on trying to qualify for the dreams and visions God gives us. But, just one meeting with God, even if we're asleep as Jacob was, can bring radical heart changes which enable us to walk in God's purposes and ways. It was with this understanding in mind that David wrote and sang Psalm 84 which contains these words:

> *"Better is one day in your courts*
> *than a thousand elsewhere;*
> *I would rather be a doorkeeper in the house of my God*
> *than dwell in the tents of the wicked."*
>
> (Psalm 84:10 NIV)

It was with the same understanding that Paul wrote under the inspiration of the Holy Spirit,

> *"Now the Lord is the Spirit, and where the Spirit of the Lord is, there is freedom. And we, who with unveiled faces all reflect the Lord's glory, are being transformed into his likeness with ever-increasing glory, which comes from the Lord, who is the Spirit."*   (2 Corinthians 3:17–18 NIV)

There is a transcending freedom which can only come from spending time in the presence of the Lord. And no amount of religious striving or effort on our parts can substitute for those intimate moments with God.

God is exalted on high, the Bible tells us, yet because of His heart of all hearts, He chooses to dwell with the lowly. Jacob was a man who was, to a degree, pretty despicable. Yet God saw the longing in his heart for Him and His love. When the established Church today looks at the younger generations – a generation of extremists – they too can often only see sinners. They see the tattoos and the pierced faces and body parts. They hear the loud demand for experience that goes beyond even what the generations of the 1960s knew. Yet, God sees a generation of Jacobs who feel like they're "second-born" in comparison to their parents' self-centeredness which the 1960s gave birth to.

It would be a bit ridiculous to try to define the move towards post-modernism which has taken place in contemporary society, in one or two sentences. However, one of the most significant characteristics that stands out about post-modernism is the cry for both structure and experience at the same time. By that I mean there is a need for structure, stability and a sense of belonging because of the almost complete lack of structure and stability they have grown up in. Too many children growing up without fathers and parents, or parents who have not known how to provide consistent morals or guidelines for life. But, along with that need for stability, there is also a definite commitment to *experience* truth. Because many of today's children have grown up with parents effected by the moral vacuum of the 1960s, they have developed a complete distrust of "accepted" formulas. Whether they pertain to economics, the media, morality, politics or religion, post-modernists are highly skeptical, and are thoroughly reluctant to accept anyone's word for anything. They will not accept black and white, closed-wall thinking. When it comes to religion and God they do not so much want to hear about God, as they want to *experience* Him.

So the Church is faced with a culture which is more and more in need of some sort of stability, but at the same time is greatly desirous of experience. These are the generation of Jacobs. They appear much like Jacob – the usurper – extremely self-centered, rude, and jostling for position. What's driving them however is not so much the selfishness of the 1970s or the 1980s for material success, but rather a longing for real relationships they can count on, with constancy and reality.

When the woman who had most likely been a prostitute cleansed Jesus' feet with her tears, hair, and expensive perfume, the religious leaders were aghast at Jesus' willingness to allow Himself to be touched by this sinner. Jesus however, defended her extravagant display. It stands to reason that a generation of Jacobs coming to God from of a place of selfishness and grasping, will, when finding the love and life their hearts actually are craving, like the prostitute in the story, break the known religious boundaries for loving God fearlessly.

We need pastors and leaders in the Church today who can see beyond the colored hair and the nose rings; who can view extreme people with God's extreme compassion. Who can disciple them from extreme selfishness to extreme selflessness? This is the type of generation that will seek God with a burning desire.

Chapter 14

Swinging Wide the Gates

In the final three verses of Psalm 24 we read,

> *"Lift up your heads, O you gates;*
>   *be lifted up, you ancient doors,*
>   *that the King of glory may come in.*
> *Who is this King of glory?*
>   *The* LORD *strong and mighty,*
>   *the* LORD *mighty in battle.*
> *Lift up your heads, O you gates;*
>   *lift them up, you ancient doors,*
>   *that the King of glory may come in.*
> *Who is he, this King of glory?*
>   *The* LORD *Almighty —*
>   *he is the King of glory. Selah"*   (Psalm 24:7–10 NIV)

There are three things that stand out in these three verses. Firstly, what are these gates that David is singing about? Secondly, for what purpose should they be opened? And lastly, why is it that someone other than the Lord Himself needs to open the gates, as the psalm suggests?

Gates and gatekeepers are two topics often mentioned in the Bible. Jesus made the great declaration in the gospel of John,

> *"I tell you the truth, I am the gate for the sheep."*
>   (John 10:7)

Obviously, He was not speaking about a physical gate, but rather that He is the only "gate" – entrance point – by which man can have access to the pastures of God (see John 10:9). But David was not speaking about Jesus, the Gate, in this passage. David is focusing on a gate that we, the people of God, can choose to open, or keep shut.

1 John 4:8 says that God is love. What that means for humanity is that the relationship, especially the *depth* of relationship, that God desires with us will always be a choice. True love never violates free will, otherwise what is offered back comes not so much from love, but fear or manipulation. So, there are spiritual "gates" that the people of God, both individually and corporately, can choose to open for God. Many ask, "How much of God can we experience in this realm?" I believe the question needs to be reversed: "How much of ourselves can we give to God"? The writer of Hebrews counsels us to,

> *"...approach the throne of grace with confidence, so that we may receive mercy and find grace to help us in our time of need."*　　　　　　　　　　　　　　　(Hebrews 4:16 NIV)

We, by an act of our wills, must open the gates of our hearts and allow God to come in. We must seek Him out and invite Him to do so. The whole premise of Psalm 24 is *"Who will* [choose to] *ascend the hill of the Lord?"* Those that will choose to do so are, in effect, seeking the face of God. And, in so doing they become a people who can open up the gates for others also. They become in effect, gatekeepers.

Obed-Edom became such a gatekeeper. He hosted the very presence of God, the Ark of God's glory, in his home for three months (2 Samuel 6). The Scriptures tell us that the presence of the Lord "blessed the family of Obed-Edom" (1 Chronicles 13:14). However, when David heard that the Lord was blessing Obed-Edom, he was incited to a godly jealousy and began to think again about bringing the Ark into the City. Obed-Edom faced a choice. Would he stay satisfied with the gifts and blessings God had given Him, or was he now addicted to the Gift-giver and willing to obey Him? Indeed he had now become a God-addict. It was impossible for him to be content merely with the blessings he had received from the Lord. Neither could he live today on the memories of God's presence yesterday. He was desperate for more of God today, so he did the only thing he could. When David came and took the Ark, Obed-Edom went with it! And we read in 1 Chronicles 15:24 that Obed-Edom became *"a gatekeeper for the Ark."*

Obed-Edom became a priest who presided over the entrance into the glory of God. Jesus, the High Priest of all high priests, is the gate Himself into the presence of God. No one can come to the Father except by Him, He stated. But there is still a need for gatekeepers today. Not gatekeepers into the presence of God, because Jesus has already opened that gate, or veil, with His blood. And certainly not religious gatekeepers who will allow some but not others into the things of God. What we need are gatekeepers who can, in effect, open up the gates of the Church and our cites to the glory of God.

Although it is of great value to have several churches in a community that love to preach and teach the Word of God, it is of even greater value to have churches and church leaders who, like Obed-Edom are caught up in their love for the Person of God. They can, as Obed-Edom did, become gatekeepers. Not gatekeepers who keep some in and others out, but gatekeepers who swing wide the gates of the Church and make it a true resting place for the presence of God. They become the friends of the Bridegroom who, like John the Baptist, prepare the way for a greater move of God's Spirit. They become like the Levites who ministered with song, instruments, oil and perfume to the very presence of God. But without these two "wings" of ministry, or even with only one of them, instead of resembling a strong and majestic eagle, the Church more resembles a chicken that is endlessly going around in circles, unable to get off the ground. We need both a heart for man and a heart for God to really become Christ-like!

But, when the church in a city begins to attract and then minister to the presence of the Lord, He begins to really show up because a resting place has been made for Him. Church history is filled with accounts of revivals which have touched entire cities and even nations with the Gospel in a comparatively short period of time. But almost always those revivals have been preceded by a small group of people who dared to believe that God had more for their culture and cities than they were currently experiencing. Typically, like the Moravians, they were men and women who were devoted to prayer and worship, as well as evangelism and ministry to the poor. But they realized that if they were going to see the fulfillment of God's great commission for their generations, they had to begin with the great commandment of loving God with all their hearts.

In effect, these forerunners could be called pre-revivalists, or precursors to revival. Or, in David's language we could say they are "gatekeepers" who swing wide the ancient doors to let in the King of Glory!

One of the wonders of getting to know God, is no matter how far into the knowledge of Him and His ways we have come, compared to yesterday, we will always have so much further to go. But, rather than it being a point of frustration, like a student struggling to master algebra, we go from glory to glory, faith to faith, blessing to blessing, and they are always new every morning. It is not a question of discovering new truths or doctrines, so much as more fully realizing and experiencing the glory of what we already have come to know in part. This is the beauty of a lifestyle centered around seeking His face. Much of the Body of Christ in the western nations have a rather one-sided revelation of Jesus. We have experienced the sweet salvation of the Lamb of God, but have seen little of the majesty and power of the Lion of the Tribe of Judah. For the sake of our nations today, we very desperately need *"the Lord, strong and mighty in battle"* to touch the churches and then our cultures.

And what of the ongoing work of the Gospel a missionary or an evangelist might ask? Should that be abandoned merely to spend more time in prayer and worship? The fact is, when we get hold of a whole lot more of God, then He has a much greater hold on us. The things we desire to do on His behalf, that were actually birthed in His heart, will become easier for us to do, not more difficult. His vision for our lives and times becomes a reality rather than a dream. A great harvest becomes a living faith, rather than a nice, but distant

hope. And we come back to what the Good News is all about
– God, His love, compassion, mercy, glory, and power. And
when we are walking in that reality, ministry becomes a joy
rather than a religious burden.

Lastly, it needs to be noted there are, in essence, two levels
of authority among gatekeepers. There are the "Obed-
Edoms" who are made up of all sorts people, of all ages, and
all areas of life. These men and women may be in church
leadership or may not be. What qualifies them to be a
gatekeeper is their adamant pursuit of the person of God.
But, there is a second type of gatekeeper, as well, who does
not so much keep the gates to the temple as Obed-Edom did,
but are more *city gatekeepers* who God has given spiritual
authority to within in the Body of Christ.

Usually, these men and women are in a senior level of
authority over a congregation or have a city-wide ministry.
Their authority is not one that can be grasped, stolen or
bought. Neither is it one that a title or diploma bestowed by
man can release. It is given in every city to a few leaders
whom God has called to be leaders in the Church of the city.
We are used to thinking of church leadership and structure in
a congregational, or single, church fellowship, sense. According to the New Testament however, God sees the "Church of
Ephesus", or the "Church of Corinth". He sees the Church
of the city, and the senior pastors of churches as collectively
acting as the elders of the city. And to these leaders God gives
authority.

This authority to be spiritual gatekeepers can be used in
both a positive sense and a negative sense. For example,
when an outside ministry, such as a well-respected evangelist, is asked by the gatekeepers of a city to come and do a
gospel outreach, there will be a much greater anointing on
the meetings simply because the gatekeepers have opened
the door for that person spiritually. I noticed in Europe, for
example, during the mid 1980s when I began to do multi-
church meetings, that there was always a greater anointing
on those meeting because of the unity amongst the gatekeepers who were collectively receiving my ministry.

Another example is when there is bad, or heretical teaching that is blowing through the Body of Christ. If the leaders

of several churches come together and recognize it for what it is, and agree not to receive this ministry or teaching in their city, there can be a great barrier which rise up to prevent the teaching from influencing the saints of that city.

However, to whom much is given much is required. Gate-keepers such as these are called to really be people of prayer and to grow in spiritual discernment. Because, often times in church history, church leaders have rejected out of hand a genuine move of the Holy Spirit, simply because they did not understand it according to their past experiences. Because they did not pray and listen to the Holy Spirit, blessings of renewal and revival have passed over those cities.

This is why there is a great need for true unity of relation-ship among leaders today. Too many leaders have rejected or dismissed other pastors in their town, simply because they belonged to a different denomination, or perhaps had differ-ing views on eschatology. We have all been guilty of majoring in the minors to such a degree that we have failed to realize that what we all have in common – the Lord Jesus Christ – actually completely overshadows our peripheral differences. The bad fruit has been divisiveness, and as Jesus said, *"a house divided cannot stand."* We have seen over the last four decades in North America how world cultures and morals have made more of an impact on the Church than vice versa. Our open door has been shut through the disunity among the gatekeepers.

It requires gatekeepers in the unity of the Holy Spirit to open up both the city-wide gates so that the glory of God can really come in. Of course, every Christian and every church that walks in the ways of God does receive blessings from God. That is a given because our Father is a good Father and He will never stop loving and caring for us. But what we have not, for the most part really experienced is the "commanded blessings" of unity.

> *"Behold, how good and how pleasant it is for brothers to*
>   *dwell together in unity!*
> *It is like the precious oil upon the head, coming down upon*
>   *the beard, even Aaron's beard;*
> *Coming down upon the edge of his robes.*

It is like the dew of Hermon coming down upon the
  mountains of Zion;
For there the LORD *commanded the blessing, life forever."*
                                    (Psalm 133:1–3 NASB)

The message for leaders today is that if we can come to together with a Christ-like attitude of preferring and blessing one another, without personal agendas and ambition, we can then, as gatekeepers for the city, come collectively to a place where the anointing and ministry of the Holy Spirit flows like oil. We can come to a place where because of unity, the weapons formed against the Church will not prevail, because there are no cracks or holes in the walls for them to enter by. But what that means is that the gatekeepers must die to personal ambition; they must die to any thought of building their own empires and become devoted to getting more of the King of Glory and His Kingdom. It is at this point that the heads of the gates the church leaders, and the Obed-Edoms, the gatekeepers of the ark, can powerfully help usher more of God into our cities.

"And we see that you are moving
A mighty river through the nations
And young and old will turn to Jesus
Fling wide you heavenly gates
Prepare the way of the risen Lord
Did you feel the mountains tremble?"
                    (Martin Smith, © 1997 Furious? Records)

Chapter 15

Holy Prophetic Frustration – the Forerunner Spirit (part 2)

"Nothing that is worth doing, can be achieved in
our lifetime, therefore we must be saved by hope.
Nothing which is true or beautiful or good makes
complete sense in any immediate context of history,
therefore we must be saved by faith.
Nothing we do, however virtuous,
can be accomplished alone,
therefore we must be saved by love."
(Reinhold Niebuhr)

"Hope deferred makes the heart sick,
but a longing fulfilled is a tree of life."
(Proverbs 13:12 NASB)

Last year most fans of sport will have witnessed, either first-hand or on TV, the spectacle of the Millennium Olympics in Sydney, Australia. Consistently, the Olympics is one of the most widely viewed televised events in all the world. Part of the great attraction of the Olympics is the patriotism – wanting to see how one's nation fares in the competitions. Part of the draw is to watch the greatest athletes in the world perform. To view the Olympics is to share in the drama and thrill of humans striving to reach the full potential of their God-given gifts. But, to rejoice with that swimmer, runner, or any of the athletes who wins the prize is to celebrate far more than merely receiving honor at that place and time. It is the celebration of a human who dared to believe an almost impossible dream. It is the celebration of years of discipline, endurance and hard work the dream demanded.

Occasionally, an Olympic athlete will be fit enough to compete in three Olympics. A rare few have gone on to four. But, for most they usually have one or two Olympics in which to put their talents to the test and achieve their dreams. For many of them, that test over a few intense days is the climax of years and years of hard work and sacrifice. Hundreds of early mornings and late night work-outs. Being forced to work at low paying, part-time jobs during hours when most of their peers are socializing or relaxing. But perhaps the biggest fight is the one that only they, their family, and their closest friends see – the fight to continue to believe in their dreams. But because they have dared to believe and dared to allow their lives to be governed by those dreams, the whole world both celebrates with the winners and agonizes with the losers.

God calls His Sons and Daughters to be to be spiritual athletes – to be His "forerunners". We are called to be a people who dare to believe dreams that will often seem extreme, if not irrelevant to the world. The problem such forerunners face however, is not so much the derision of the unchurched, but the criticism of the churched! Part of the problem with western Christianity is that we have made many "believers" in Christ as opposed to "disciples" of Christ. If there is one chief trait that stands out in both the life of a successful athlete, and a successful follower of Christ, it is *discipline*. It is not for nothing that we're called to be "disciples".

The difference between a believer and a disciple is simply that one "disciplines" himself for a higher calling, while the other does not. They can both share the same mindset and theology, but one will allow that mindset to dominate his/ her heart, lifestyle and choices, while the other does not.

The apostle Paul, in his first letter to the church of Corinth wrote,

> *"Do you not know that in a race all the runners run, but only one gets the prize? Run in such a way as to get the prize."*
> (1 Corinthians 9:24 NIV)

Basically, there are two types of footraces – there are sprint distances and there are races in which the runner must pace himself over a longer distance, rather than running all out from the beginning. A sprint calls for a great burst of speed for a very short period of time. A longer run calls for one to pace oneself along with strategic bursts of speed. A marathon however, the longest of all races, traditionally 26 miles long, calls not only for speed, but a steady pace of endurance for hours. While there are seasons in all things, including our lives, the race that God calls His people to, is a lifelong marathon, rather than a few short sprints that are quickly over. Even as Olympic athletes compete for their nations, so we are called to run for the Kingdom of God. We are, in fact, called to run in such a way that the nations will be given to Christ as His inheritance.

It is easy for us to become involved in short-term causes, which, like a short race, one can put a comparatively high amount of energy into for a short period of time. Causes such as prayer for a season, specific evangelistic outreaches, good works and church projects etc. But, for many when they finish that specific work or project, it is back to "business as usual". The forerunner, however, is like the marathon runner. He or she, endures the early mornings and late nights because they are willing to adapt their lifestyles to the goal of the prize, and they are willing to make lifelong choices governed by a determination to pursue their dream.

In the western culture of today, the normative values which seem to have emerged in the last few decades mostly revolve around instant gratification without any sense of personal responsibility. We see this illustrated in the parallel rise of sex without commitment to relationship, and the tremendous increase of unwanted babies. The incredible increase in frivolous lawsuits, the amount of theft stores suffer from their own workers, the growing lack of commitment to family values, all point to a deeply entrenched self-centeredness. We are a culture today in which we want to do what we want, when we want, and have someone else pay the bill. The generations in their fifties and older, look at the younger generations with both askance and incredulity.

Unfortunately, the Church can also become affected with the same mindset and value systems of the world when it does not heed the more costly instructions of the Bible. In fact, there are many churches today that pride themselves on growth methods focused on "low thresholds" into the Church family. There is much to be said for lowering the bar as far being sensitive to cultural styles, which are often neither right nor wrong. But, when churches tend to measure themselves by the size of the crowd they draw, rather than their impact for the Kingdom of God on the culture around them, something is seriously out of alignment. To a large degree this is part of the problem with the effectiveness of the Church in changing our nations – we have traded the basic disciplines of the Bible for comfortable Christianity. As my friend, the Rev. Mark Hoffman says,

> "You can find God anywhere in the universe except for one place. You can never find Him in your own personal comfort zone."

What we need today in the Church are long-term dreamers. I do not mean day-dreamers, rather Christians, churches and church leaders who are willing to pay the price to pursue long-term dreams. Often when an Olympic athlete decides to become an Olympic athlete, he or she is a very young man or women. Often they are not even in their teens yet. But as they begin to understand not only the talent they have, but the potential of that talent, they begin to dream dreams which will dominate the next a decade or two of their life.

John the Baptist was set aside from birth because of God's call on his life to "prepare the way". Luke tells us that,

> *"The child grew and became strong in spirit, and he lived in the desert until he appeared publicly to Israel."*
>
> (Luke 1:80 NIV)

The deserts of Judea and Israel that John and Jesus frequented, like the lonely isles the Celtic saints spent time on, were synonymous with prayer, worship, and being set aside for the Kingdom of God. Often the men and women

God has used to usher in a move of the Kingdom of God have been people of such focus. They forsook marriage and the possibility of a family and home, because they were gripped by their long-term dreams and visions. In no less than five passages of the New American Standard translation of the Bible, it records either Jesus privately, or with His disciples, withdrawing to a "lonely place". The lonely places are places without the constant distraction of people, computers, videos, stereos and telephones. They are completely devoid of distraction and entertainment, but they are places to go and be alone – alone with God!

Men and women who are gripped by long-term dreams, such as Jesus and John the Baptist, such as the apostles, such as the early Celtic saints who Thomas Cahill credits as saving civilization, such as a young athlete working towards an Olympic games happening eight years from now, all have one thing in common. They know that the greater the goal, the greater the price tag. And those price tags are at tremendous odds with today's insatiable quest for instant gratification.

Long-term, unrealized goals are hard to live with. As Solomon wrote in the book of Proverbs,

"Hope deferred makes the heart sick."   (Proverbs 13:12)

Dreams and visions that remain unrequited for too long can cause one to despair and settle for mediocrity. Or, they can further toughen a person to become even more resolved and focused. It is far too easy for church leaders today to make decisions that have cheap short-term costs, rather than very expensive long-term price tags. We need Christians and leaders today that are willing to daily act on dreams and visions that may only have long-term pay-offs. We need leaders who are willing to pick up their cross and choose to walk lonely roads that may be far away from the popularity of instant gratification.

Those of us who consider themselves followers of Christ, of all people should be willing to walk the "road less traveled". After all, we are the ones who believe that as wonderful as this life can be, it is but a shabby reflection of what's to come. The apostle Paul in his epistle to the church of Rome wrote,

> *"I consider that our present sufferings are not worth comparing with the glory that will be revealed in us."*
> (Romans 8:18 NIV)

The dilemma of contrasting present-day costs with eternal payoffs is a little like the rhetorical question, "We all want to go to heaven, but who wants to die right now?"

I believe personal revelation of the glory of God and His purposes are essential if we are to really run the long race. Abraham and Sarah were willing to leave everything behind because of the personal revelation God gave them of the promises to come. Jesus was willing to leave the Father's right hand, come to earth, live as a mere human, and give His life in pain, humility and rejection, because He knew *"he had come from God and was returning to God"* (John 13:3). The apostle Paul was willing to embrace a life in which it was prophesied he would suffer much, because of the surpassing revelations he experienced of Jesus. It is one thing for our mindsets to be changed by good biblical theology, but for our lifestyles to be freed from the common and petty dictates of the 21st century, we need our hearts to be captured by a revelation of God – the author of life, Himself.

For this reason a true forerunner is not so much a sprinter, who can win a prize by a few short bursts of speed and energy, but a long-distance runner who is willing to persevere through the tedious and lonely workouts with the finish line nowhere in sight. The ethos of the long-distance runner must be like that of the heroes of the faith such as Abraham, Moses, David and Gideon –

> *"Faith is being sure of what we hope for and certain of what we do not see."* (Hebrews 11:1 NIV)

> *"Therefore we do not lose heart. Though outwardly we are wasting away, yet inwardly we are being renewed day by day. For our light and momentary troubles are achieving for*

us an eternal glory that far outweighs them all. So we fix our eyes not on what is seen, but on what is unseen. For what is seen is temporary, but what is unseen is eternal."

(2 Corinthians 4:16–18 NIV)

Chapter 16

The Spirit of Prophecy

"One thing I ask of the LORD,
this is what I seek:
that I may dwell in the house of the LORD
all the days of my life,
to gaze upon the beauty of the LORD
and to seek him in his temple."
(Psalm 27:4 NIV)

"The real voyage of discovery consists not in seeking
new landscapes but in having new eyes."
(Marcel Proust)

In the last chapter I stated that it was more because of personal revelations of God than good intentions, that induced people like Abraham, Moses and others, to run the lifelong races they ran. The experience of revelation and the deposit which it leaves often makes a far deeper impact on our lives than simply understanding principles of preposional truth. In this final chapter of the book I want to remind us again what our ultimate goal in pursuing open heavens is – essentially, to know more of Jesus! And I also want to examine the role of revelation and prophecy on our quest to discover more of Him.

For many, the desire for a prophetic dream or vision foretelling what is to come, stems from a desire to know their future blessings – such as where they are to live, what they are to do, and/or their future financial prosperity. Our true riches and inheritance of course are not mansions, streets of gold, or even crowns. Neither are they rewards that can be measured by the yardstick of money, or materialism. Our true riches are not, so much the gifts God gives, but rather the Gift-giver Himself – the Person of God. And, as was the case with many in the Bible, when we begin to experience true revelation of His glory, rather than being caught up in our own purposes and agendas, we become deeply propelled into His will for our lives.

Isaiah was projected into a phenomenal prophetic ministry that is still having a great impact on God's people today. This happened as he experienced the dramatic revelation of the presence of God. Isaiah was filled with remorse as he gazed on the holiness of God and realized how short he and the rest of humanity fell. In another sense he was crying out "I'm undone! What good am I now!" because he had just seen the one sight which would render all others in his life worthless by comparison. All of a sudden, all the commonplace visions and goals which in themselves were probably good, fulfilling, even wonderful, must have seemed so trivial in comparison to the wonder he had just gazed upon. And even though a crown of life is promised to those who overcome, we read of the 24 elders of Israel in John's revelation, laying down their crowns at the feet of the True Prize – Jesus (Revelation 4:10).

The apostle Paul wrote to the church of Philippi,

"But whatever was to my profit I now consider loss for the sake of Christ. What is more, I consider everything a loss compared to the surpassing greatness of knowing Christ Jesus my Lord, for whose sake I have lost all things. I consider them rubbish, that I may gain Christ and be found in him ... "   (Philippians 3:7–9 NIV)

The Greek word used in verse 8 which the New International Version translates as "rubbish" can be more fully understood by looking at the King James translation which uses the word "dung". Paul is making a powerful and dramatic comparison here in which his purpose is not so much to devalue everything else, but rather to illustrate that the value of truly knowing God is so far superior to any other knowledge.

I remember one experience with a young student at a Bible school in Europe where I had been speaking for a few days. I was speaking on the topic of intimacy with God. In the final session we had been having a time in the class of waiting on the Lord to hear what He might have to say. This particular young man was already involved in leadership and ministry. In fact, his father and grandfather had been pastors and leaders in the Pentecostal Church movement in Sweden. As we spent some half an hour waiting and listening in our hearts for the Holy Spirit, the young man was weeping most of the time. As the session came to a close I asked him to share what the Lord might be saying to him. What he went on to say made an indelible imprint on my soul. He sobbed, "I've just seen Jesus, what am I supposed to do with my life now?"

It wasn't that the goals and visions he had for his life and ministry were not good goals. For that matter, they were possibly God-given goals. But all of a sudden, via revelation, he realized the true goal was not numbers, crowds, publicity, noise, or any outward success – it was the person and glory of the Lord Jesus Christ! Everything else, no matter how good, paled by comparison. It is possible, if not probable, that for much of the western Church our knowledge of the glory of God is primarily intellectual. It has been perceived as a religious, poetic, or theological reality as opposed to an experiential reality. The fact is, however, that all of humanity is rapidly approaching a day when all knees are going to bend and all heads are going to bow in the acknowledgement and revelation of that all-consuming glory. The question for the contemporary Church is, "If Jesus stated in His prayer to the Father that He has already given His glory to His people (John 17), then why aren't we experiencing the reality of it more?"

The necessity and purpose of prophecy

There are many supernatural gifts God desires to give the Church. The list mentioned in 1 Corinthians 12 includes the gifts of healing and miracles. All of them are given to the Church for the purpose of building the Church. They are the workman's tools God gives us for extending His Kingdom. Essentially however, Paul stated prophecy was the gift to especially seek after (1 Corinthians 14:1).

In Paul's description of the use of the gift of prophecy, at least in the corporate church setting, he says that it is to be used to strengthen, comfort and edify (1 Corinthians 14:3). Furthermore, Paul makes it clear that, although there are those called to the office of the prophet (Ephesians 4:11), all can, as the Spirit works, prophesy (1 Corinthians 14:31). We understand, by the obvious implications of the word *prophecy*, that while the purpose of prophecy is to strengthen, comfort, edify, instruct and encourage, that by very definition prophecy has to do with *foretelling*. That means to give insight into what is to come.

It is vital that the modern-day prophets of Christ's Church speak from a position of real intimacy with Him. If they are to give insight into the future shape of the Church; if they are to encourage and edify it in real terms, then they must surely have a balanced perspective based on a real revelation of Jesus.

We have within the Church, many Bible teachers and preachers who can speak quite eloquently on the topic of grace from a solid biblical perspective. But, in some of those same ministries the church members are motivated by fear and manipulation from the said leader, rather than grace and encouragement. In short, it can be said, a Christian can know truth about Jesus, but come up short on knowing the Truth Himself. In the same manner, a prophet, or prophetically gifted person can also reveal things that are to come, but fail to help the people to see the Truth Himself which is to come – Jesus!

A Holy Spirit inspired word concerning future events and blessings can be of enormous help to an individual, or even a church, in turning a corner and coming into the fresh things God is breathing forth. In fact, often where there is a lack of the prophetic, resulting in a lack of vision, the present good becomes the enemy of the future great. Isaiah wrote,

"See, the former things have taken place, and new things I declare; before they spring into being I announce them to you."   (Isaiah 42:9)

As was the case with Samuel first encountering the future king Saul (1 Samuel 9) or the prophet Agabus prophesying the apostle Paul's future arrest (Acts 21), prophecy does have to do with future events, blessings and situations. However, seeing future events are really only a *part* of prophecy, rather than the *heart* of prophecy.

Just as Jesus is not merely *a truth* of the Bible, but *the Truth Himself*, so the *heart of prophecy is the revelation of the Person of Jesus*. What an evangelist is to the unsaved – a person who can show them Jesus – so should a prophet be to the Church. He or she should be someone who can, as David put it in Psalm 34:3, "Magnify the Lord" (NASB) for the people of God. The prophetic is intended to help us adjust the lenses of our hearts so that we see God more as He truly is.

Rob Critchley, one of the worship pastors at Toronto Airport Christian Fellowship in Canada, wrote a worship song that, in a nutshell, magnifies the Lord Jesus. That is, the song helps the worshipper realize that God is so much larger than we think. The song is appropriately titled *Great Big God*. The song, as the title indicates, sings of a great big God and also by way of comparison, mentions a "little bitty devil". And although the song does not plumb the depths of theological truth, it does very powerfully help the worshipper take a simple biblical truth in their head and transport it into their heart where it begins to have a more direct influence on their daily life, attitudes and outlook. Prophecy along with prophetically anointed worship and times of prayer is a gift from the Holy Spirit that enables us to more accurately see God as He truly is and respond to Him as such. The apostle Paul prayed for the church of Ephesus that,

"The God of our Lord Jesus Christ, the glorious Father, may give you the Spirit of wisdom and revelation, so that you may know him better. I pray also that the eyes of your heart may be enlightened . . . "   (Ephesians 1:17–18 NIV)

If we were to do a thorough biblical examination of the main themes of the major prophets of the Bible, there is one theme that consistently stands out. That is the glory and wonder of the Person of God. This can be seen in the Old Testament prophets such as David,[1] Elijah, Isaiah, Jeremiah, Ezekiel, and Daniel. For example we read in Daniel 7:13–14,

> *"In my vision at night I looked, and there before me was one like a son of man, coming with the clouds of heaven. He approached the Ancient of Days and was led into his presence. He was given authority, glory and sovereign power; all peoples, nations and men of every language worshiped him. His dominion is an everlasting dominion that will not pass away, and his kingdom is one that will never be destroyed."* (NIV)

When we examine the themes of the two major prophets of the New Testament – John the Baptist and the apostle John – we see an overriding theme of the glory of the Person of God. For example we read in Matthew 3:11 of John the Baptist's prophecy:

> *"But after me will come one who is more powerful than I, whose sandals I am not fit to carry."*

Even more telling is John's heartcry for Jesus found in the John chapter 3. His disciples have brought to his attention the dilemma that this man, Jesus, whom John had prophesied was to come, is now becoming the new darling of the people. The crowds who were up to then coming out to listen to John were now following Jesus. This was, most probably, presenting a practical problem as well, since in all likelihood John's financial support was decreasing due to the shift of the crowds. John's response was the stirring proclamation and prayer, *"I must decrease, but He must increase."*

The apostle John who had seen everything there was to see in two generations of church life and the prolific spread of the Gospel was locked up in exile on the Isle of Patmos at the end of his days. But there he experienced a whole new, fresh revelation of the glory of Jesus that caused him to be filled with fear and wonder all over again. He records this vision of Jesus in Revelation 1.

> *"I turned around to see the voice that was speaking to me. And when I turned I saw seven golden lampstands, and among the lampstands was someone 'like a son of man,' dressed in a robe reaching down to his feet and with a golden sash around his chest. His head and hair were white like wool, as white as snow, and his eyes were like blazing fire. His feet were like bronze glowing in a furnace, and his voice was like the sound of rushing waters. In his right hand he held seven stars, and out of his mouth came a sharp double-edged sword. His face was like the sun shining in all its brilliance. When I saw him, I fell at his feet as though dead."* (Revelation 1:12–17 NIV)

Perhaps, one of the most startling and clear Bible passages which illustrates this emphasis on the glory of the Person of God is found towards the end of John's revelation in chapter 19. In verse 11 John is conversing with an angel who states *"Blessed are those who are invited to the wedding supper of the Lamb."* The greatest honor and blessing is not so much the privilege of walking streets of gold for evermore, rather it is being invited to the wedding of the Lamb – the Son of God! But it is verse 12 however, which really keys us in. As John begins to give adoration to the angel, who certainly would have appeared powerful and glorious in comparison to man, the angel rebukes John for doing so. He says to John,

> *"Do not do it! I am a fellow servant with you and with your brothers who hold to the testimony of Jesus. Worship God! For the testimony of Jesus is the spirit of prophecy."*

Prophecy, dreams, visions, insights into what is to come – all can be beneficial. After all, God has created us to journey in this life as pioneers. And when the road both behind and ahead is dark, or uncertain, it is certainly encouraging to see light at the end of the tunnel. But as exciting as those insights, or God-given dreams may be, our ultimate goal should always be the Person of God rather than the things of

God. The greatest level of prophetic insight is never so much to do with the things which are to come, but rather the Person Who is to come and the growing revelation of His glory on the face of the Earth.

We can identify with Peter who, along with James and John, ascended the mountain with Jesus as recorded in Matthew 17. All of a sudden Jesus was transformed into a fragment of His true glory. Along with Him, Moses and Elijah also appeared in glorified forms. Certainly, they did not make an appearance as long dead mummies from an ancient tomb! In the excitement of the event Peter offered to build three tabernacles for them (Matthew 17:4 NASB). In the midst of Peter's sense of awe and excitement, the Father spoke out of a cloud of glory to Peter and said,

> *"This is my Son, whom I love; with him I am well pleased. Listen to him!"* (Matthew 17:5)

God the Father was not only speaking out His approval and love for His Son, but was also instructing the disciples not to get lost in the experience of the revelation, but to keep their eyes and ears focused on the Person of Jesus. At that point they became filled with fear and fell on the ground face first. Afterwards Jesus then raised them up and encouraged them not to be afraid. Verse 8 reads,

> *"When they looked up, they saw no one except Jesus."*

The immediate fruit of their revelation on the mountain was that thereafter, they only had eyes for Jesus. We need such a prophetic stirring in the Church today. We need the stirring of the Holy Spirit over the waters of the Church to wake us up from our introspection and self-centeredness. We need prophecy, but we need a higher form of prophecy to bring us back to that essential and foundational first love of God. It's only as the eyes of our hearts are truly focused on God that we can begin to see others, and even ourselves as He sees us. It is only as we begin to really gaze on His heart that we can have His heart for humanity. This is the call today on the Church – not merely to experience the prophetic, but to be a prophetic people who have "ears to hear what the Spirit is saying to the church." Then, and only then, will we experience the open heavens of God's awesome and amazing power.

> *"Then I looked and heard the voice of many angels, numbering thousands upon thousands, and ten thousand times ten thousand. They encircled the throne and the living creatures and the elders. In a loud voice they sang: 'Worthy is the Lamb, who was slain, to receive power and wealth and wisdom and strength and honor and glory and praise!' Then I heard every creature in heaven and on earth and under the earth and on the sea, and all that is in them, singing: 'To him who sits on the throne and to the Lamb be praise and honor and glory and power, for ever and ever!' The four living creatures said, 'Amen,' and the elders fell down and worshiped."*   (Revelation 5:11–14 NIV)

Note

1. According to Acts 2:30 David was viewed as a prophet, as well as a king, worshipper, artist, and warrior.

If you have enjoyed this book and would like to help us to send a copy of it and many other titles to needy pastors in the **Third World**, please write for further information or send your gift to:

Sovereign World Trust
PO Box 777, Tonbridge
Kent TN11 0ZS
United Kingdom

or to the '**Sovereign World**' distributor in your country.

Visit our website at **www.sovereign-world.org**
for a full range of Sovereign World books.